THE ULTIMATE BRAIN HEALTH LOGIC
PUZZLE BOOK FOR ADULTS

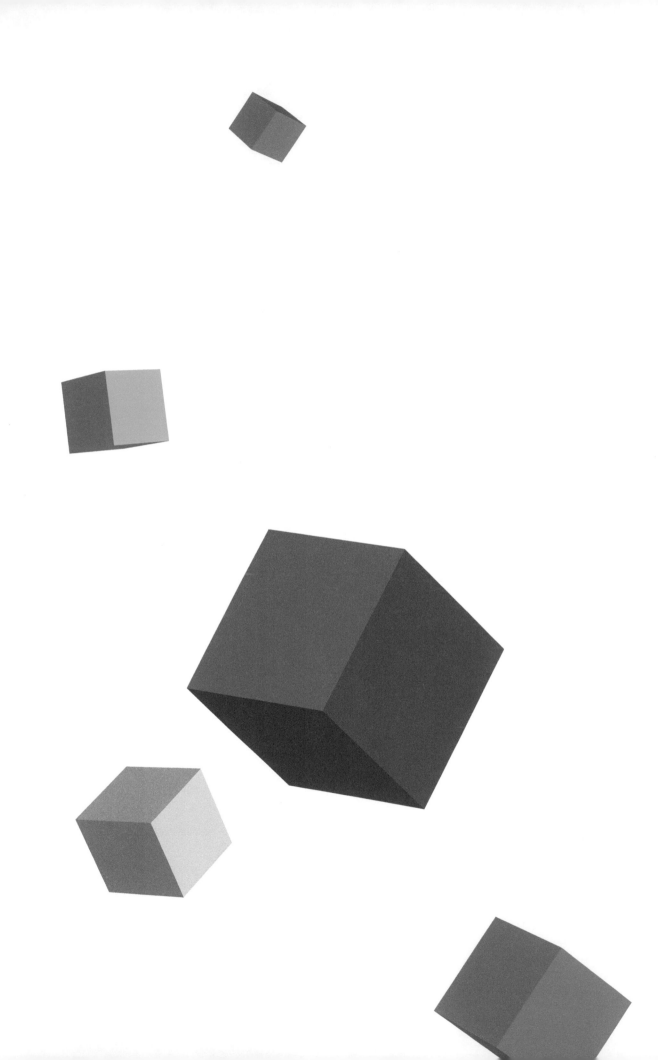

THE ULTIMATE BRAIN HEALTH LOGIC PUZZLE BOOK

FOR ADULTS

Sudoku, Calcudoku, Logic Grids, Cryptic Puzzles, and More!

Marcel Danesi, PhD

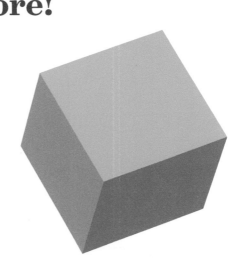

ROCKRIDGE PRESS

Series Designer: Darren Samuel
Interior and Cover Designer: Stephanie Sumulong
Art Producer: Hannah Dickerson
Editor: Annie Choi
Production Editor: Ashley Polikoff
Production Manager: Martin Worthington

Puzzle Grids © 2021 Collaborate Agency

ISBN: 978-1-63807-037-5
R0

CONTENTS

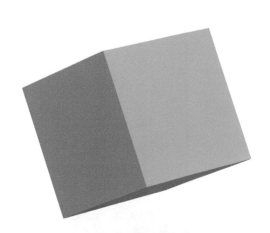

WELCOME!

As a very young person, I came across a puzzle that stuck with me ever since for both its simplicity and ingenuity. It was devised by the 16th-century mathematician Niccolò Tartaglia: A father dies, leaving 17 camels to be divided among his heirs, in the proportions ½, ⅓, ⅑. How can this be done? Dividing up the camels in the manner decreed by the father would mean having to split up a camel. This would, of course, kill it. So, Tartaglia suggested "borrowing an extra camel," for the sake of argument, not to mention humane reasons. With 18 camels, he arrived at a practical solution: one heir was given ½ (of 18), or 9, another ⅓ (of 18), or 6, and the last one ⅑ (of 18), or 2. The 9 + 6 + 2 camels, given out in this way, add up to the original 17. The extra camel could then be returned to its owner.

How truly clever and "logical." Tartaglia's strategy certainly solves the situation logically, though whether or not it is a legal solution is another matter. Whatever the truth, the fascinating thing to me has always been that the solution is satisfying in itself. It is "its own reward," as the British puzzlist Henry E. Dudeney so aptly put it about puzzles in general.

I have been composing logic puzzles for several decades, continuing to be fascinated by the mixture of simplicity and ingenuity of thinking that they exhibit. I even taught a first-year undergraduate course on puzzles at the University of Toronto for many years, which allowed me to transmit the power and beauty of logic puzzles to students. That is my objective with this book as well—to transmit the unique appeal of logic puzzles to you, the reader. They require no specialized training, just the activation of logical thinking that is in all of us, perhaps lying dormant there.

In this book, you'll find six different logic puzzles: sudoku, calcudoku, logic grids, masyu, nonograms, and cryptic puzzles. As an academic, I was at first skeptical that puzzle solving could truly enhance brain functioning. But after so many years of being engaged with puzzles practically and academically, I am no longer a skeptic. Puzzles are designed to play (literally) on the brain's multiple systems and this is likely what makes them so effective and appealing. Adding puzzles into your daily routines may be an effective way to keep the brain functioning at full tilt and thus remain healthy throughout life. Puzzling is chicken soup for the brain!

Do not worry if any of these puzzles are unfamiliar to you. I will explain each type in this warm-up chapter. As you go through the book, you will find that the puzzles become increasingly tricky, from easy (chapter 2) to medium (chapter 3) and difficult (chapter 4). But they are still solvable in the same way as the warm-up puzzles. Occasionally, you might have to use a little bit of "lateral logic," as did Tartaglia with his camel puzzle. The techniques used to solve the logic puzzles in this book can, actually, be employed to enhance, rehearse, and sustain logical thinking in general. Enjoy!

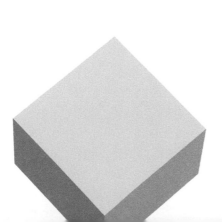

WARM-UP

GETTING STARTED WITH SUDOKU

Brain-Health Benefits

Working on sudoku puzzles can strengthen your deductive reasoning and attention to detail. Prefilled numbers are valuable clues for you to determine whether there is only one possible number to fill a cell. To make this determination, you must employ a systematic analytical approach, which is a good deductive reasoning exercise. It is also important to focus on details. Many times (to my chagrin), I have found myself in a blind alley. How did I get there? Usually, I failed to recognize a number embedded in a clump of other numbers when I surveyed the sudoku grid.

How to Solve

To solve a 9x9 sudoku puzzle, fill in each cell with a number from 1 to 9 so that each row, column, and 3x3 "cage" contains each number, with no repeats. There can be only one possible solution.

To get started, scan the puzzle for each digit, starting with 1, to see if there are enough of them so that you can fill in the rest. Then look for the rows, columns, or cages that have five or more numbers filled in to see if you can deduce where the others can be placed—with no guessing! After you have explored these possibilities, once again scan the puzzle for each number. This will give you a good starting point to test out hypotheses on number placement to solve the rest of the puzzle.

SUDOKU 1

ANSWER ON PAGE 116

	3	6	4		1	7	2	8
8		9	3	2	7	5		1
1		7	5		6	9		4
3	8	1		6	5	4	7	
	9		1	7			8	5
7		5	8		2	1	9	3
6		8		5	4	3	1	
	1	4	7				5	6
2	5				1	9	8	7

GETTING STARTED WITH CALCUDOKU

Brain-Health Benefits

Working on calcudoku puzzles can strengthen your deductive reasoning skills, creative thinking, and short-term memory because it requires you to use all three throughout the activity. A player approaches a calcudoku puzzle by using creative thinking to develop possible solutions and then testing them. Testing your hypotheses gives your short-term memory a workout. Being able to play one, two, and three moves ahead is how you play this game and solve a calcudoku puzzle.

How to Solve

To solve the calcudoku puzzle, fill each empty cell in the grid with a number 1 through 4 (or 5, 6, or 7, depending on the size of the grid) so that each row (across) and column (down) contains all of the numbers, with no repeats. The cells of the grid are arranged in "cages" of two or more cells. Each cage has a small number and arithmetic symbol in the upper-left corner as a clue to which numbers belong there. For example, a clue of 3+ in a two-cell cage means that the two numbers added together should equal 3. Single-cell cages simply designate the number that belongs there.

In cages with three or more cells that require subtraction or division, you perform the calculation for each of the smaller possible numbers against the largest number. For example, if the clue for a three-cell cage is "1÷" and you deduce that 6, 3, and 2 would fit in the cage, you would test your answer like so: 6÷3 = 2; 2÷2 = 1. Voilà!

To get started, first fill in any single-cell cage and look for cages for which there can be only one answer, such as a three-cell cage in a straight line that gives the clue 6+, since the only possible numbers can be 1, 2, and 3.

CALCUDOKU 1

ANSWER ON PAGE 116

5+		3	16x
3	6x		
		3-	
7+			3

GETTING STARTED WITH LOGIC GRIDS

Brain-Health Benefits

The logical reasoning involved in solving these puzzles activates several processes: elimination, inference, and deriving unique conclusions from given facts. These puzzles also graft common-sense knowledge into the logical admixture: for example, a mother is older than her children, an only child has no brothers or sisters, and so on. In my estimation, the greatest benefit to be gained from logic grids is setting in motion the brain's coordination of given information with everyday facts.

It would seem that the brain understands information best by comparing it to other information and to everyday experience—and that is exactly what these puzzles do. They present facts that can only be understood in terms of other facts in the puzzle, comparatively and contrastively, as well as in terms of common sense.

How to Solve

A logic grid puzzle starts with a statement such as this one: "Sheena, Maria, and Darlene majored in chemistry, computer science, and history, but not necessarily in that order." The puzzle will then give you other bits of information so that you can establish which person majored in which discipline, among other things. The key to solving these puzzles is to eliminate possibilities until there is only one left under each category. For example, if "Maria did not major in chemistry," you would eliminate this possibility for her. If told that "Sheena majored in computer science," then we can establish that it was Darlene who majored in chemistry, since she is the only one left under that category.

Each puzzle comes with a logic grid, which allows you to keep a visual tally of your deductions and eliminations. To check off invalid possibilities, fill in the relevant cell with an *X*. Using the example above, you would write an *X* in the cell that connects "Maria" and "chemistry," thus eliminating this possibility. In the other example, you could write an *O* in the cell that connects "Sheena" and "computer science" and an *X* in each of the cells that remain for that category—vertically and horizontally, thus eliminating it as a possibility for the other women. You will then see an empty cell under "chemistry" for Darlene.

In addition to the given grid, creating a summary chart like the one below can help for more complex puzzles:

NAME	PROFESSION	FLAVOR

PUZZLE ON NEXT PAGE

LOGIC GRID 1

Ice-Cream Friends

Jamila, Rosie, Gary, and Desean are good friends. One is a doctor, another a dentist, a third a lawyer, and a fourth a computer programmer, but not necessarily in that order. They meet every Friday afternoon at an ice-cream parlor to enjoy one another's company. Each friend always has the same flavor of ice cream—chocolate, vanilla, cherry, and pistachio—again, not necessarily in that order.

Can you match each friend to their profession and favorite ice-cream flavor based on the given facts?

1. Jamila and the doctor do not like the chocolate ice cream, and never intend to order it.

2. Neither Gary nor Desean is the dentist or the lawyer.

3. The programmer, Jamila, and Gary live in the same condo building.

4. The programmer is the one who orders the chocolate ice cream.

5. The doctor is not the one who orders the vanilla or cherry ice cream.

6. Rosie and the lawyer work in the same office complex. She hates vanilla.

ANSWER ON PAGE 116

	DOCTOR	DENTIST	LAWYER	PROGRAMMER	CHOCOLATE	VANILLA	CHERRY	PISTACHIO
JAMILA								
ROSIE								
GARY								
DESEAN								
CHOCOLATE								
VANILLA								
CHERRY								
PISTACHIO								

GETTING STARTED WITH MASYU

Brain-Health Benefits

Masyu is a dot-connecting puzzle that is useful for developing spatial reasoning. It involves envisioning how the dots can be connected in specific ways to produce the correct path around the grid. Masyu thus activates visualization processes, which are controlled mainly by the right hemisphere of the brain—the so-called "visual hemisphere." Visual puzzles are very important for activating the cells in this hemisphere, because these cells then activate cells in other areas.

How to Solve

Masyu is played on a rectangular grid of squares, some of which contain one of two kinds of circles, either white (empty) or dark (filled). The objective is to draw a single continuous straight line that passes through all circled cells. The line must enter each cell it passes through from the center of one of its four sides and exit from a different side.

- For white circles, the line must travel straight through, but it must turn 90 degrees through one or both of the adjacent cells, or beyond. The line can pass through other circles before turning. It can go through a row of circles, all of which can turn in subsequent cells.

- For dark circles, the line must turn 90 degrees and pass straight through both adjacent squares.

MASYU 1

ANSWER ON PAGE 116

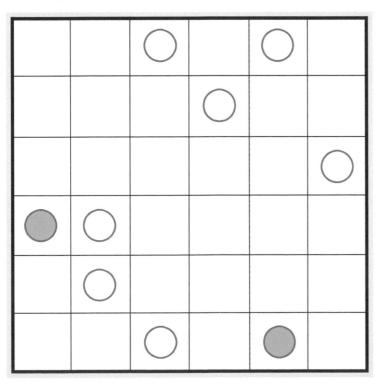

GETTING STARTED WITH NONOGRAMS

Brain-Health Benefits

I recall vividly one class at the university in which I introduced a simple nonogram to the students in order to illustrate how logic and visualization converge in this type of puzzle. One student immediately refused to do it because, she claimed, she was not good at this sort of thing. I left it at that. But at the next class she came up to me and thanked me. She ended up doing the puzzle at home successfully, impressing upon herself that she could, in fact, reason and visualize at the same time. Nonograms are marvelous activators of these two fundamental processes in the brain.

How to Solve

Nonograms are picture logic puzzles in which the cells in a grid must be shaded or left blank according to the number clues provided on the top and on the left side of the grid. The objective is to reveal a hidden picture in the grid by applying the number clues to the grid logically.

The title of each nonogram is a clue as to what figure is hidden within it. If the title is "cat," then the image hidden in the grid is that of a cat. Keep in mind that the figures are not representational as in a true painting or drawing. They consist of pixelated dark cells and are thus a visual approximation, not an exact representation.

Most nonograms can be solved a single row or column at a time; you then try another row or column—repeating this trial-and-error process until the puzzle is complete. Start with number clues that are easily figured out. For example, a clue of "2 3" means that there are two and three cells to be shaded, in that order, with one blank cell between them. In a five-by-five grid, this clue allows you to solve a row or column easily—the first two cells are shaded, the next one is blank, and the last three are shaded. If a clue is not helpful at some point, come back to it later, working on other clues and thus other parts of the grid.

NONOGRAM 1

Robot Shape

ANSWER ON PAGE 116

	1	1 2	3	1 2	1
3					
1 1 1					
3					
1 1					
0					

GETTING STARTED WITH CRYPTIC PUZZLES

Brain-Health Benefits

We are fascinated by mysteries, secret codes, and hidden patterns. When these are revealed, through a flash of insight, the reaction we tend to have is characterized as an "aha" experience, as psychologists call it—a feeling of satisfaction and wonderment at once. This leads us to cryptic puzzles, in which there is a hidden message that will be unraveled by first solving a puzzle—a sudoku, a calcudoku, and so on.

How to Solve

Cryptic puzzles may be based on logic, trivia, or wordplay, but for this book, I'm focusing on logic-based challenges. There are two distinguishing characteristics of cryptic puzzles. First, each puzzle solves to a short word or phrase; second, the cryptic method of extracting this hidden message changes from puzzle to puzzle, and it's up to you to figure it out! I've based many of these cryptic puzzles on the other five puzzle types found in this book, so those puzzle-solving skills should help you here as well.

For example, if a cryptic puzzle is based on a sudoku puzzle, you will be given letters in some cells rather than numbers. First, solve the puzzle and then relate the letters to the numbers. This will reveal the hidden message. For the warm-up puzzle, you will be told what the code is in the title.

CRYPTIC PUZZLE 1

Numbers for Words!

ANSWER ON PAGE 116

	1	4	3	7	8	6		5
7	5	3	4		9		2	1
6	8		5	1	2	7	...M	4
8		5		...I	6	1	4	
1	9		7	4	3	5	8	2
...P	7	2	8	5	1		6	3
3	2	...S	6	8	...L	4	7	9
9		8			7	2		...E
	6	7	2	9		3		8

Hidden Word: ⬚ ⬚ ⬚ ⬚ ⬚ ⬚

2

EASY PUZZLES

SUDOKU

	9	7	1	8		6	5	2
2		1	9		5		3	7
3	5	6		7	2	1		8
	2	9	5	4		8	6	3
7		5	8		9			
8	3	4		1		9	7	5
	4	3	6		8	7	2	1
6		8	3	2	1			9
5	1	2			4		8	

ANSWER ON PAGE 116

DID YOU KNOW?

The brain's two hemispheres work best when they work together. Puzzle solving is one of the activities that has been found to activate both hemi-spheres in tandem, thus enhancing overall brain func-tioning and health.

9		8		4	5		3	6
	3	2	9	8		5	4	
4	1		3		6	7		9
2	6	7		9	8	3		4
1			6		2	8	9	
8	9	3	7	1			5	2
3	8		2	6		4	7	5
	2	1		5	3	9		
	4	6	8		9	1		3

ANSWER ON PAGE 116

TRIVIA CHALLENGE

Which three countries have the highest populations?

	9	3	7	2		5	6	1
	7	1	9	5				4
5		4		1	6	9		8
7		6		3	1		2	9
4	8	9	2			6	1	
3	1		6	8			5	
9	3		1	4	2		8	6
	6	7	8			3	1	5
1		8	5		7	3	9	

ANSWER ON PAGE 116

4		5	1	8		3	2	7
1		7	5		9		6	
8	6	2		4	7			1
	1		4	7	2		5	9
9	5		8	3			4	
		4	6		5	1		8
2		3	7		4	9	1	5
6	4				8	2	7	
	7	9	2	1		4		6

ANSWER ON PAGE 117

SUDOKU

06

	6	4	5		2	1	3	
	9	3		1	6	2		
2		1		4	3	5		6
3		6		2			5	1
9			3	7	1		8	2
1	2		6	5		3		7
4	3		1	9		8		5
	1	9	4			5	7	3
6			2		8	9	1	4

ANSWER ON PAGE 117

07

7	4	2	1			3		8
		9	8	7	5	1		2
1	8				3	9	7	6
3	6	1	7	2			9	4
		4	9					
9		8		1	4	2	6	
4		3		9	2	7	8	5
5			4			6	3	9
8	9	6	3	5	7			1

ANSWER ON PAGE 117

TRY THIS!

Pair puzzle solving with other physical activities to boost overall fitness. One easy activity is walking, which increases cardio-vascular fitness and boosts endurance.

TRIVIA CHALLENGE

What is the largest bone in
the human body?

			5	7	9			3
6	1			4	8			
		3	6	1			5	4
1	8				7	2	9	5
4		7	9	8			6	1
	5	9	2	6	1	7		
2			8	9	4		3	7
5	3	4	7			1	8	9
9		8	1	5				6

ANSWER ON PAGE 117

CALCUDOKU

7+	6x		
	7+	4x	4
12x			2

ANSWER ON PAGE 117

DID YOU KNOW?

How good are you at spotting patterns? The ability to spot patterns is controlled by cell structures in the brain that activate pattern recognition. Doing puzzles stimulates those cells, helping you seek out any patterns in front of you.

1	24x	5+	
2÷			
	12x		5+
6x			

ANSWER ON PAGE 117

04

7+			12x
3+	6x		
		3	7+
1-			

ANSWER ON PAGE 117

05

1	24x		
12x		6+	
	4	8+	
			4

ANSWER ON PAGE 117

CALCUDOKU

3+	1	9+	3
			4÷
4	10+	2	
3			

ANSWER ON PAGE 117

DID YOU KNOW?

The brain can generate new brain cells at any age. This discovery has been made possible by new and powerful brain imaging technologies, which take pictures of the brain as it performs under certain conditions. Puzzle solving is one of those conditions that generates new cells, no matter how old you are.

LOGIC GRID 2

Recent Graduates

Four students—Maria, Shamila, Jasmine, and Katia—are recent graduates of the same university, having majored in mathematics, history, Spanish, and physics—in no particular order. Their last names are—again, in no particular order—Bramish, Hoskins, Norabella, and Wang.

Given the following information, can you match the students to their surnames and majors?

1. Neither Maria nor Ms. Bramish majored in math. Shamila also did not major in math.

2. Jasmine majored in physics.

3. Shamila and the history major belonged to the same sorority.

4. Incidentally, Ms. Wang is the one who majored in history.

5. Jasmine and Ms. Hoskins, who majored in Spanish, knew each other in high school.

ANSWER ON PAGE 117

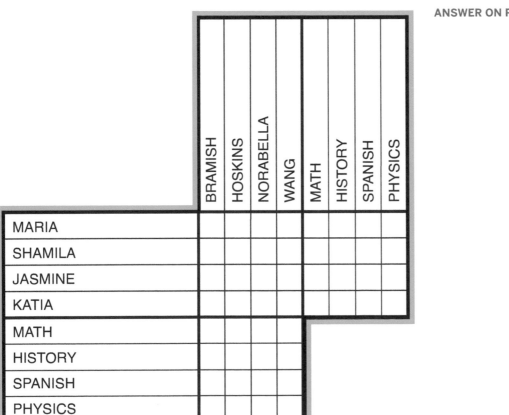

	BRAMISH	HOSKINS	NORABELLA	WANG	MATH	HISTORY	SPANISH	PHYSICS
MARIA								
SHAMILA								
JASMINE								
KATIA								
MATH								
HISTORY								
SPANISH								
PHYSICS								

LOGIC GRID 3

Colorful Night Out

Four friends always meet up on Saturday night to play card games. Their names are Paula, Marco, Heather, and Jamil. For some strange reason, each person always comes dressed with the same-colored shirt—green, blue, white, yellow (but not necessarily in that order). Their ages are 25, 30, 55, and 70 (again, in no particular order), showing that age does not matter in true friendship.

Can you match each person with their age and favorite shirt color based on the given facts?

1. The oldest in the group wears the white shirt.

2. The youngest wears the yellow shirt.

3. Paula is neither the youngest nor the oldest, but she is older than Marco, who is also not the youngest.

4. Heather does not wear either the green or white shirt.

5. The green shirt wearer is not 55 years old.

ANSWER ON PAGE 117

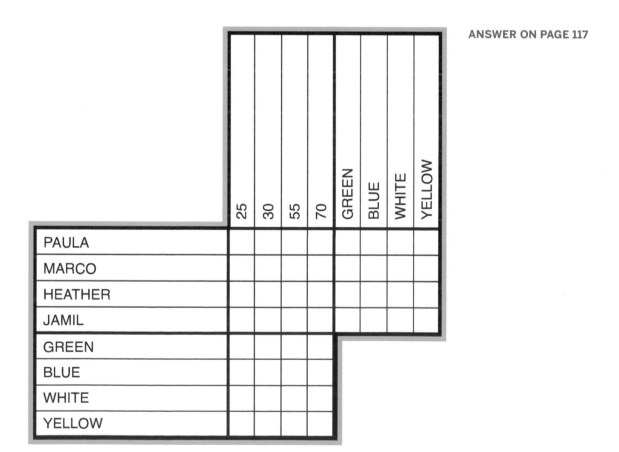

LOGIC GRID 4

Great Deals

An electronics store recently held a sale of four popular items—a laptop, a sophisticated mobile device, a popular video game, and a computerized watch. A clerk at the store was preparing to put price tags on them—$100, $250, $500, and $705 (not necessarily in the order just described). Each item came with a special offer—a free lifetime warranty, a further discount, a free ticket to a ball game, or a free supply of batteries (again, in no particular order).

Given the following information, can you match each item with its price tag and the bonus it comes with?

1. The laptop is neither the cheapest nor the most expensive of the four items.

2. The laptop is more expensive than the watch, which is not the cheapest of the four either.

3. The mobile is also not the cheapest.

4. The bonus that came with the most expensive item was the ticket to the ball game, and with the cheapest, a further discount.

5. The laptop did not come with a lifetime warranty.

ANSWER ON PAGE 117

	100	250	500	705	WARRANTY	DISCOUNT	TICKET	BATTERIES
LAPTOP								
MOBILE DEVICE								
GAME								
WATCH								
WARRANTY								
DISCOUNT								
TICKET								
BATTERIES								

LOGIC GRID 5

International Competition

Four athletes—a gymnast, a long-distance runner, a wrestler, and a swimmer—competed at an international meet last week, winning the four medals of the competition—gold, silver, bronze, and platinum. Each athlete came from a different country to participate in the competition—Italy, Zambia, Slovakia, and Greece (in no particular order).

Based on the following information, can you figure out which athlete won which medal, and what country each athlete came from?

1. The gymnast, the gold medal winner, and the athlete from Italy stayed in the same complex.

2. The runner, who was not the gold medalist, became close friends with the athlete from Greece.

3. The swimmer and the athlete from Italy won the bronze and platinum in some order.

4. The athlete from Slovakia did not win the gold or silver.

5. The runner did not win the bronze, and the gold medalist was not from Greece.

ANSWER ON PAGE 117

	GOLD	SILVER	BRONZE	PLATINUM	ITALY	ZAMBIA	SLOVAKIA	GREECE
GYMNAST								
RUNNER								
WRESTLER								
SWIMMER								
ITALY								
ZAMBIA								
SLOVAKIA								
GREECE								

LOGIC GRID 6

Precious Coin Auction

Four precious ancient coins were auctioned off yesterday at a major public event. One was an ancient Roman coin, another a Greek coin, another still a Sumerian coin, and a fourth a Chinese coin. The values of the coins were, in some order, $1 million, $2 million, $3 million, and $4 million. Four buyers eventually got one coin each. The buyers came from four different countries—France, Algeria, Peru, and Belgium.

Given the following information, can you match the coins to their auction price and to the countries of their buyers?

1. Neither the Roman nor the Greek coin went for the $4 million.

2. The buyer from France spent $3 million.

3. The Chinese coin was sold for less than $3 million, but it was not the cheapest.

4. The buyer from Algeria spent the most.

5. The buyer of the Roman coin did not spend the least; the buyer from Belgium did.

ANSWER ON PAGE 118

	$1 MILLION	$2 MILLION	$3 MILLION	$4 MILLION	FRANCE	ALGERIA	PERU	BELGIUM
ROMAN								
GREEK								
SUMERIAN								
CHINESE								
FRANCE								
ALGERIA								
PERU								
BELGIUM								

LOGIC GRID 7

Vintage Cars

At a recent automobile exhibit, prizes were given for the best refurbished vintage cars. The winners of the first four prizes were cars of the 1950s—a Dodge, a Chevrolet, a Studebaker, and a Ford. Each car won, in part, because of its classic color—blue, green, black, and silver (in no particular order).

Can you figure out how each car placed (first, second, third, or fourth) and what color it was, based on the following information?

1. Neither the Dodge, the black car, nor the blue car came in first.

2. The Dodge, the Chevrolet, and the blue car were owned by the same person.

3. The green car did not come in either third or fourth.

4. The Chevrolet placed either second or third.

5. The Ford, which was silver, did not place fourth.

ANSWER ON PAGE 118

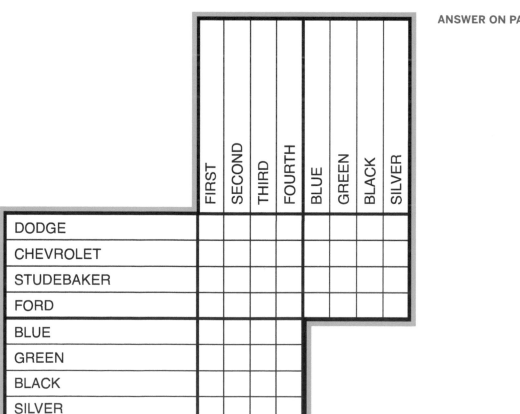

LOGIC GRID 8

Medical Associates

Four young medical practitioners work in the same building complex, making it easier to refer patients to one another according to each case. Their names are Paula, Kayla, Derek, and Leroy; and their surnames are Garcia, Sanji, Gorski, and Troy, but not necessarily in that order. Their specializations are cardiology, podiatry, neurology, and urology (again, in no particular order).

Given the following facts, can you match the practitioners with their surnames and their specializations?

1. Paula, Kayla, and the cardiologist regularly go out to dinner on weekends.

2. Neither Derek nor Dr. Gorski is the cardiologist; Dr. Sanji is neither the podiatrist nor the urologist.

3. Derek, the podiatrist, and Paula have their offices on the same floor.

4. Derek, Dr. Troy, and Dr. Sanji have known one another since high school.

5. Dr. Troy is neither the neurologist nor the podiatrist.

ANSWER ON PAGE 118

	GARCIA	SANJI	GORSKI	TROY	CARDIOLOGY	PODIATRY	NEUROLOGY	UROLOGY
PAULA								
KAYLA								
DEREK								
LEROY								
CARDIOLOGY								
PODIATRY								
NEUROLOGY								
UROLOGY								

LOGIC GRID 9

Coffee and Sweets

Four longtime friends—Nakia, Darlene, Kamira, and Shauna—meet up every Saturday morning at their favorite pastry shop. Each one always orders the same coffee (in no particular order)—espresso, Americano, mocha, and macchiato—and the same pastry (again, in no particular order)—croissant, Danish, strudel, and éclair.

Can you figure out what type of coffee each person drinks and which pastry each one eats at the Saturday morning get-together, given the following facts?

1. Neither Nakia nor Darlene orders the espresso or croissant.

2. The person who orders the mocha also orders the éclair.

3. Kamira orders either the mocha or the macchiato.

4. Nakia, Kamira, and the mocha drinker live near one another.

5. Shauna is not the one who has the croissant.

6. The Americano drinker always has the Danish.

ANSWER ON PAGE 118

	ESPRESSO	AMERICANO	MOCHA	MACCHIATO	CROISSANT	DANISH	STRUDEL	ÉCLAIR
NAKIA								
DARLENE								
KAMIRA								
SHAUNA								
CROISSANT								
DANISH								
STRUDEL								
ÉCLAIR								

26 THE ULTIMATE **BRAIN HEALTH LOGIC PUZZLE BOOK** FOR ADULTS

LOGIC GRID 10

Tennis Pairs

Four friends, Tamika and Brenda, Juri and Nimish, frequently get together on weekends to play a tennis match in pairs (always with the same partners). The players wear distinctive animal logos on their T-shirts—a lion, a tiger, a bear, and a deer (in no particular order). They also use different types of tennis rackets, called power, control, tweener, and modern.

Can you match each player to the logo and racket type based on the following information? Also, can you figure out who the pairs were?

1. Tamika's partner wears the lion logo and uses a tweener racket.

2. Juri is not Tamika's partner. He does not wear the bear logo.

3. The one who uses a power racket is the one who wears the bear logo.

4. Juri's partner wears the deer logo and uses a modern racket.

5. Nimish does not wear the lion logo.

ANSWER ON PAGE 118

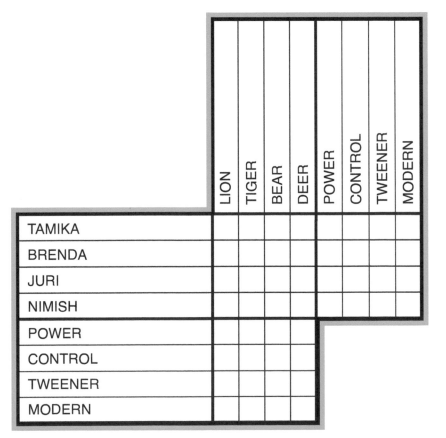

LOGIC GRID 11

Basketball Mania

Four high school basketball teams made it to the semifinals in a national competition, attended by many enthusiastic students across the country. The teams came from high schools in Austin, Chicago, Tulsa, and Reno. The teams finished first, second, third, and fourth in some order. The names of the four coaches were Maria, Jake, Blaise, and Kristina (in no particular order).

Can you figure out who coached each team and how each team placed, based on the following facts?

1. The Austin team came in either first or fourth. Jake's team placed third.

2. Maria's team and the team from Chicago placed second and third (in some order).

3. Blaise's team and the team from Tulsa came on the same flight.

4. The Reno team placed second or third.

5. Kristina's team did not place first.

ANSWER ON PAGE 118

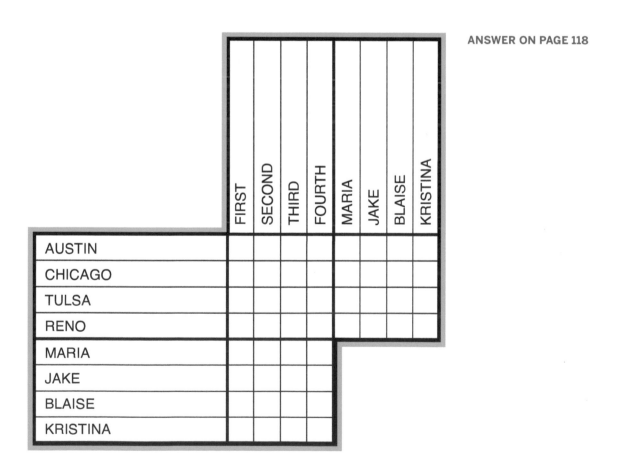

LOGIC GRID 12

Household Companions

Gurdeep, Lana, Keshawn, and Pina live on the same street and each has a household companion that they love—a dog, a cat, a gerbil, and a turtle (not necessarily in that order). Strangely, each animal will fall asleep at night only by listening to a particular genre of music—jazz, classical, rock, or rap.

Given the following facts, can you match each person with their pet and each animal to the music it falls asleep to?

1. Gurdeep's companion, which is not the dog nor the gerbil, does not fall asleep to either jazz or classical.

2. Lana's companion, which is also not the dog, falls asleep to either jazz or rap.

3. The turtle, which is not Keshawn's companion, does not fall asleep to rock.

4. Pina's companion, which is not the gerbil, does not fall asleep to jazz.

5. The dog, which is not Keshawn's companion, falls asleep to rap.

ANSWER ON PAGE 118

	DOG	CAT	GERBIL	TURTLE	JAZZ	CLASSICAL	ROCK	RAP
GURDEEP								
LANA								
KESHAWN								
PINA								
JAZZ								
CLASSICAL								
ROCK								
RAP								

MASYU

02

ANSWER ON PAGE 118

DID YOU KNOW?

Doctors are increasingly recommending puzzles as a way of improving "mental flexibility," or the ability to respond quickly and correctly to changing circumstances by reasoning.

03

ANSWER ON PAGE 118

TRY THIS!

If you are having difficulty solving a particular puzzle, let it go for a bit. Come back to it later, and you will likely find that the mental cobwebs have cleared and you can attack it anew.

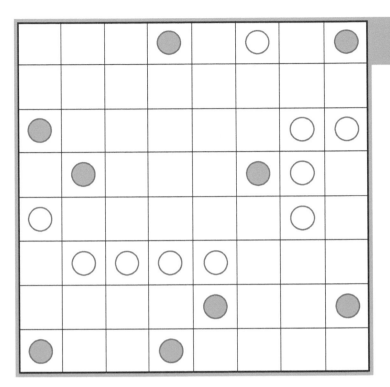

ANSWER ON PAGE 118

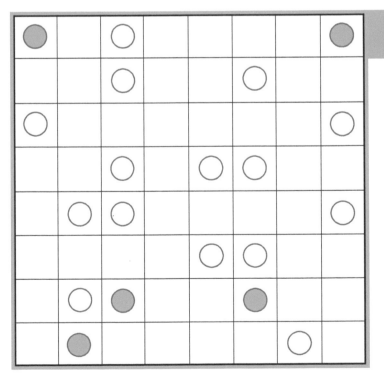

ANSWER ON PAGE 118

Easy Puzzles 31

MASYU

ANSWER ON PAGE 118

TRIVIA CHALLENGE

What continent is the largest one, constituting nearly one-third of the landmass of the earth?

NONOGRAM

Information Technology

	4	0	1	4	1
0					
1 3					
1 1					
1 1					
1 1					

ANSWER ON PAGE 118

Crossing Stairs

	1 1	1 1	1	1 1	1 1
1 1					
1 1					
1					
1 1					
1 1					

ANSWER ON PAGE 119

NONOGRAM

A Matching Pair

	1	3	1 1	3	1
2					
1					
2 2					
1					
2					

ANSWER ON PAGE 119

A Column Bridge

	1	3	1	3	1
0					
1 1					
5					
1 1					
0					

ANSWER ON PAGE 119

A High-Rise Building

	1	3	4	3	1
1					
3					
3					
5					
0					

ANSWER ON PAGE 119

Opposing Magnets

	0	2 2	1 1	2 2	0
3					
1 1					
0					
1 1					
3					

ANSWER ON PAGE 119

NONOGRAM

Dripping Water Tap

	0	5	1	2 1	0
3					
1 1					
1					
1 1					
1					

ANSWER ON PAGE 119

DID YOU KNOW?

Aging has a negative impact on short-term memory, but there are various ways to help reverse memory loss. Research on doing sudoku and the other types of logic puzzles included in this book has been encouraging in this area.

CRYPTIC PUZZLE 2

What This Is All About

The letters of the hidden word are on the side of the calcudoku puzzle. To figure it out, you will have to solve the puzzle first.

E	4x		6x	
M	5+			4
G	2x	6+		8+
A		3		

Hidden Word: ☐ ☐ ☐ ☐

ANSWER ON PAGE 119

TRIVIA CHALLENGE

Which organ in the body has the highest blood flow?

CRYPTIC PUZZLE 3

A Physical Game Instead!

The letters in this easy masyu puzzle contain a hidden word, which you can decipher after solving the masyu first.

A	(B)	L	●
O	D	G	L
(E)	L	L	●
V	Y	H	I

Hidden Word: ☐ ☐ ☐ ☐ ☐ ☐ ☐ ☐ ☐ ☐

ANSWER ON PAGE 119

TRIVIA CHALLENGE

Can you name the three components of an atom?

CRYPTIC PUZZLE 4

The Order Matters

The solution to this logic grid puzzle conceals a hidden word regarding something the friends are all into. Figure it out after solving the puzzle.

Six friends—Artemis, Ahmed, Keisha, Reina, Ella, and Troy—decided to go to the corner movie theater on Saturday afternoon, a throwback to the golden era of movie watching. When they got there, the theater had not opened up yet and there was no one else there. In line with movie tradition, they decided to line up, one after the other, waiting for the theater to open its doors. Here's how they did so.

1. Neither Artemis nor Ahmed was the first in line.

2. Reina is behind Keisha and Artemis but before Ahmed and Troy.

3. Ella is just behind Troy.

4. Troy is just behind Ahmed.

5. Artemis is just behind Keisha.

	FIRST	SECOND	THIRD	FOURTH	FIFTH	SIXTH
ARTEMIS						
AHMED						
KEISHA						
REINA						
ELLA						
TROY						

Hidden Word: ☐ ☐ ☐ ☐ ☐ ☐

ANSWER ON PAGE 120

CRYPTIC PUZZLE 5

It's a Start!

Solve the puzzle like you would any nonogram, and then see if you can figure out what the hidden word is.

	5	1	5	0	5
1 1 1	V	B	A	N	B
1 1 1	T	E	S	N	F
3 1	R	Y	N	I	H
1 1 1	S	G	C	N	K
1 1 1	J	I	D	G	L

Hidden Word: ☐ ☐ ☐ ☐ ☐ ☐ ☐ ☐ ☐

ANSWER ON PAGE 120

CRYPTIC PUZZLE 6

It Comes Out at Night!

Solving the calcudoku puzzle provides the key to unraveling the secret code that will allow you to discover the hidden two-word phrase.

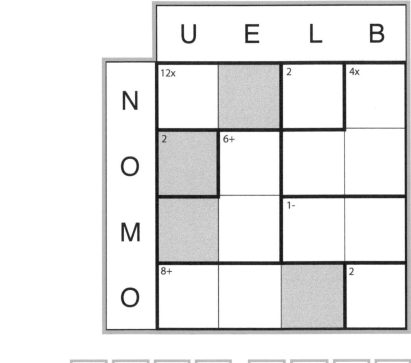

Hidden Words: ☐ ☐ ☐ ☐ ☐ ☐ ☐ ☐

ANSWER ON PAGE 120

CRYPTIC PUZZLE 7

As in the previous masyu cryptic, the solution to the puzzle will allow you to discover the hidden word. By the way, this masyu is a bit harder than the other ones in this chapter.

A	B	D	C	A	N	S
Q	T	R	V	Y	W	X
A	N	S	D	L	T	M
O	K	E	K	L	P	N
W	U	I	R	R	P	P
V	Y	U	O	I	L	Y
L	A	R	D	U	S	

Hidden Word: ⬚⬚⬚⬚⬚⬚⬚⬚⬚⬚⬚

ANSWER ON PAGE 120

CRYPTIC PUZZLE 8

Fun Place to Be on a Sunny Day

Here's another logic grid puzzle that conceals a hidden word. You can unravel that word only after solving the puzzle and using the answers to do so.

Four people—Becky, Angela, Lina, and Letisha—are 23, 24, 25, and 25 years of age, but not necessarily in that order. Each one has a job as painter, artist, researcher, or karate instructor—again, not necessarily in that order.

Can you figure out the age and job of each person based on the following information?

1. Becky, the artist, and the researcher live near one another.

2. The karate instructor lives far from everyone.

3. The painter is the youngest of the four, and the karate instructor the oldest.

4. Angela, Lina, and the karate instructor went to the same high school.

5. Lina is older than the artist.

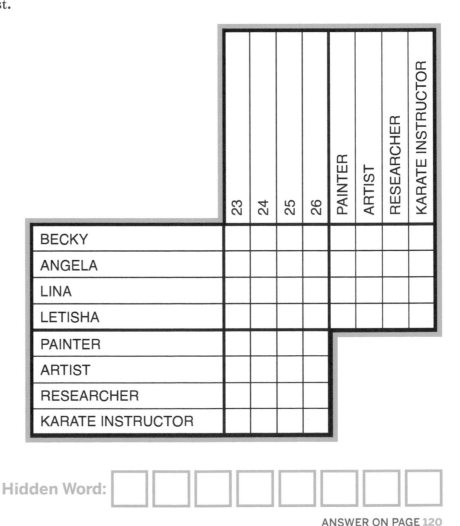

Hidden Word:

ANSWER ON PAGE 120

3

MEDIUM PUZZLES

SUDOKU

09

	3	2	4		6	1		9
	6		1	2	3		8	4
4		1		7		3	6	
9	4		7		2	8	1	5
	1	7			5		3	
6		5		1		9		7
2		4	8	3	7		9	1
	7	6		9		4		
1	9			5		7	2	3

ANSWER ON PAGE 121

10

4	7			6	5	3		2
1	5			8	2	7		4
2	3	6	9			8		
	4	5	2			9	8	
		3	5	9	4	6	2	
9		2	8		3			5
6		7	4	5	1			9
3	9			2		5		
5	2			3	9	4	7	8

ANSWER ON PAGE 121

TRY THIS!

Once you have finished a chapter, or the whole book, start over and redo all the puzzles. You might be surprised to find that you may not remember how you solved them in the first place, but that you are better at solving them the second time around.

TRIVIA CHALLENGE

What color does litmus paper turn when it is dipped in an acid?

ANSWER ON PAGE 121

ANSWER ON PAGE 121

SUDOKU

13

1		3	4		7		6	2
	5	4		2	1	8		
7	2			6	8	4	1	3
8			1	5	9			6
	6	1			3			
3	9					1	5	4
9			2			6	8	1
	7	8	9	1		3		
4			8	3		2		7

ANSWER ON PAGE 121

14

4		6	2		9	3		7
	3		4		1		6	
8	2		7	3		9		4
		8			4	7	9	1
2	7	1	8					3
6			3	1	7	8	5	
5		3	1			4	7	9
	6	7	9			5		
9	4			7	8	1		

ANSWER ON PAGE 121

TRY THIS!

Make a list of the five puzzles that gave you the greatest difficulty. Put the list aside for a while. Come back to it later and attempt the puzzles again. This will increase "mental fluency," or an enhanced ability to think logically and creatively at once.

Puzzle 15:

				7	1	9	3	4
5	3	7	4	9				6
	4	1	2	6				7
	9	2	3	5				1
4	8				7	5	6	
1	5				4	3	7	2
3	2			1	5	6	4	8
8				3				5
6	1			4	9	7	2	

ANSWER ON PAGE 121

16

Puzzle 16:

		2	6	8			5	4
		5			3	1		9
8	9	3			4	7	6	2
5	2				6	4	9	
9			8	4				5
4	6	8	9		5			7
7	1	6			8	5	4	
					7	9		1
		9	4	3			7	6

ANSWER ON PAGE 121

CALCUDOKU

9+		7+	3	6+
48x				
		200x	4+	
3x				
5		1-		4

ANSWER ON PAGE 121

15+	4	6x		
			4	15x
2	6x	4		
12x			5	12+

ANSWER ON PAGE 122

TRIVIA CHALLENGE

About how many pounds does an adult human brain weigh?

18x			7+	5
5	60x			
11+				6x
		4		
1	7+		12x	

ANSWER ON PAGE 122

7+	14+		3	20x
			1	
	8x	3	8+	
2-				5+
	5	4x		

ANSWER ON PAGE 122

CALCUDOKU

11

16x	20x			9+
		2-		
15x	8+	4	4x	
	3	40x		

ANSWER ON PAGE 122

ANSWER ON PAGE 122

DID YOU KNOW?

The brain is a lifelong learning organ that continues to function through diverse and rich sensory and intellectual experiences. Puzzles can enhance such experiences, sharpening the mind, improving memory, and keeping the brain fit throughout life. Puzzles are to the brain what physical exercise is to the body.

12

12+	12x		30x	1
		2		
		8+		12+
6x	100x		3	

LOGIC GRID 13

Computer Geeks

Four young computer programmers work for the same Silicon Valley company. Their first names are Helena, Francine, Quisha, and Kana, and their surnames are Darah, Moore, Soto, and Lee, but not necessarily in that order. Each one is into films of a specific genre—comedy, spy, thriller, and horror. And each one is an aficionado of a particular sport—hockey, tennis, golf, and swimming.

Can you match the names and surnames of the women, as well as which film genre and sport each one is into, based on the following information?

1. Kana, Ms. Darah, and the hockey fanatic always arrive at the same time to work.

2. Kana is not into tennis or golf.

3. Ms. Moore and Ms. Soto are into either hockey or golf, in some order.

4. Helena, Francine, and Ms. Lee are not into comedies at all.

5. The comedy lover is not into hockey or tennis.

6. Quisha and Ms. Soto go out together regularly.

7. Helena and the hockey aficionado graduated from the same college.

8. Ms. Darah and Ms. Soto are not into spy movies. Helena is not into horror movies.

ANSWER ON PAGE 122

LOGIC GRID 14

A Meeting of Minds

Four renowned researchers met recently at an international conference on current ideas in the world of science. Their last names are Adebe, Gemelli, Kang, and Aetos. Their areas of expertise are in the fields chemistry, physics, biology, and medicine, but not necessarily in that order. To cope with the stress of their work, each one has a hobby—chess, checkers, gardening, or painting (again, in no particular order). Each scientist discussed their research at a roundtable in some order—first, second, third, and fourth.

Can you figure out which field each scientist is in, which hobby each one practices, and in what order they discussed their work at the roundtable, based on the following information?

1. Neither Dr. Adebe nor Dr. Aetos nor the chemist spoke first at the roundtable.

2. Dr. Kang is not the chemist. He did not speak second.

3. Dr. Adebe is a good friend of the biologist, who spoke second.

4. The chemist and the biologist are into either chess or checkers, in some order.

5. Dr. Kang is not into painting. The one who is spoke fourth.

6. By the way, the one who spoke fourth is the physicist.

7. Dr. Aetos is not into chess.

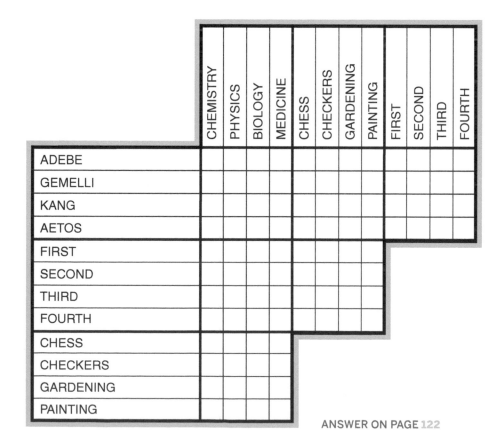

	CHEMISTRY	PHYSICS	BIOLOGY	MEDICINE	CHESS	CHECKERS	GARDENING	PAINTING	FIRST	SECOND	THIRD	FOURTH
ADEBE												
GEMELLI												
KANG												
AETOS												
FIRST												
SECOND												
THIRD												
FOURTH												
CHESS												
CHECKERS												
GARDENING												
PAINTING												

ANSWER ON PAGE 122

LOGIC GRID 15

Skating Champions

Patricia, Fiona, Frank, and Rashon are ice-skating champions. Each has won several international awards. Each skater always dons the same color for good luck—blue, red, gold, or silver (in no particular order). Each one also plays an instrument rather well—piano, violin, guitar, or cello (again, in no particular order). Each one also has a secret craving for either candy, peanuts, chips, or tarts (again, in no particular order).

Can you match each skater with their good-luck color, instrument played, and secret craving, according to the following facts?

1. Patricia does not wear the blue suit; she also does not play the cello or the piano.

2. The one who plays the piano always dresses in red.

3. The cello player always dresses in gold and loves candy.

4. Fiona does not dress in red and does not love peanuts.

5. Rashon does not play the piano and also does not eat peanuts, being allergic to them.

6. Fiona, the cellist, and the chips lover went to the same school.

7. The one who loves tarts does not wear the gold suit.

8. The one who plays the violin gets along well with Patricia and the chips lover.

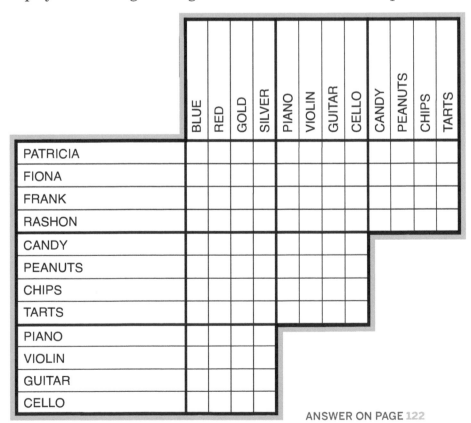

ANSWER ON PAGE 122

LOGIC GRID 16

Excellence in Sports

Four teams from the same Boston-area high school placed first nationally in their respective sports last year—baseball, football, soccer, or basketball. Each team belonged to a different year—freshman, sophomore, junior, or senior. The coaches—Ms. Williams, Ms. Chu, Ms. Lopez, and Ms. Arnand—also won awards for their outstanding coaching. Each team has a specific name—Jets, Stars, Suns, and Rockets.

Can you match each team to its name, year, and coach, given the following information?

1. Neither the freshman team nor the basketball team was coached by Ms. Williams.

2. The soccer team and the freshman team were called either the Jets or the Stars, in some order.

3. The baseball team was not coached by Ms. Chu, who was actually the coach of the freshman team.

4. The basketball team was not called the Rockets.

5. The Suns were neither sophomore nor junior teams.

6. Ms. Chu's team was not called the Jets.

7. Ms. Arnand did not coach the Jets or the Rockets.

8. Ms. Williams did not coach the Rockets, and Ms. Lopez did not coach the junior team.

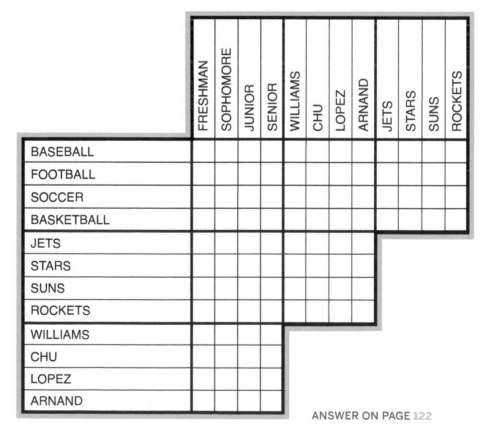

ANSWER ON PAGE 122

LOGIC GRID 17

The Arts

Four friends—Bertha, Shuping, Jamara, and Ines—are into the arts—sculpture, painting, music, and ceramics, but not necessarily in that order. Each artist speaks a language other than English fluently—Russian, Greek, French, or German, in some order. And each person has become an expert dancer in one of these four styles—tango, swing, waltz, and samba.

Can you match each person to their art, language spoken, and dance style, given the following facts?

1. Bertha, Shuping, and the sculptor meet for coffee every Thursday night.

2. The sculptor and Jamara are into either the tango or the waltz, in some order.

3. Shuping is not into swing.

4. The sculptor does not speak Russian or Greek.

5. Ines does not speak French.

6. Jamara, the painter, and the musician have known one another since elementary school.

7. Bertha and the painter each have a sister.

8. Ines and Jamara speak Russian or German, in some order.

9. The German speaker and the tango dancer live near each other.

10. The musician and the Greek speaker have very long hair.

ANSWER ON PAGE 122

LOGIC GRID 18

Card Sharks

Four friends—Katia, Sarah, Jovan, and Sam—love to play cards. Each one is brilliant at either poker, spoons, blackjack, or rummy (in some order). While playing, each person exhibits a particular "tell"—a nose wiggle, a head scratch, an earlobe touch, or a side glance. For good luck, each person always wears a specific item—a hat, a scarf, a bracelet, or a thumb ring (in no particular order).

   Given the following information, can you match each person to their card game expertise, tell, and item worn for good luck?

1. The one who excels at poker does not scratch their head or touch their earlobe.

2. The one who is brilliant at spoons also does not scratch their head or wear a scarf.

3. Katia and Sarah wear either a bracelet or a thumb ring, in some order.

4. The hat wearer and Jovan excel in either blackjack or rummy, in some order.

5. Sarah and the spoons whiz are the exact same height.

6. Jovan and the head scratcher live in the same condo complex.

7. Neither the scarf wearer nor the expert at rummy wiggle their nose.

8. The poker whiz does not wiggle their nose or wear the bracelet.

	POKER	SPOONS	BLACKJACK	RUMMY	WIGGLE	SCRATCH	TOUCH	GLANCE	HAT	SCARF	BRACELET	RING
KATIA												
SARAH												
JOVAN												
SAM												
HAT												
SCARF												
BRACELET												
RING												
WIGGLE												
SCRATCH												
TOUCH												
GLANCE												

ANSWER ON PAGE 122

LOGIC GRID 19

Avid Travelers

Four siblings—three sisters, Doreen, Anita, and Kayla, and one brother, Justin—love to travel to different places, either to Europe, Asia, Africa, or Australia (in some order). Each one is interested in a particular area of the culture—art, music, cuisine, or fashion. Strangely, each one will travel only during one of the seasons—in winter, spring, summer, or fall (again, in no particular order).

Can you figure out to which place each sibling loves to travel, what form of culture interests each one, and during which season each sibling travels, given the following facts?

1. Doreen does not travel in either winter or spring.

2. Anita does not travel in either spring or summer.

3. The sibling who travels in the spring loves to go to either Asia or Africa.

4. The spring traveler is one of the three sisters.

5. The art lover, who does not travel in the spring or fall, is also one of the three sisters.

6. Neither Kayla, the sister who loves Europe, nor Justin is into cuisine.

7. The one who is into fashion will not travel in the summer or the fall.

8. The cuisine lover goes to either Europe or Australia, but not in the fall or winter.

9. The music lover is not the one who goes to Asia.

	EUROPE	ASIA	AFRICA	AUSTRALIA	ART	MUSIC	CUISINE	FASHION	WINTER	SPRING	SUMMER	FALL
DOREEN												
ANITA												
KAYLA												
JUSTIN												
WINTER												
SPRING												
SUMMER												
FALL												
ART												
MUSIC												
CUISINE												
FASHION												

ANSWER ON PAGE 122

LOGIC GRID 20

Skilled Labor Required

A condo building has been undergoing renovations and repairs. Four skilled workers—Harriet, Bill, Jason, and Medina—have been hired for the work. One is an electrician, another a plumber, a third a carpenter, and a fourth a house painter (but not necessarily in that order). Each was born in one of the following cities—Atlanta, Dallas, Miami, or Shreveport—and loves to read a certain type of literature—fiction, poetry, drama, or biography.

Can you match each person to their skilled job, city of birth, and favorite type of literature, given the following facts?

1. Harriet is older than the electrician. She is not into poetry.

2. The carpenter is older than both Harriet and Bill.

3. Jason is not the youngest; the plumber is. Jason is not from Miami.

4. Medina, who is the oldest, Harriet, and the electrician get along with the one from Miami.

5. The electrician is not from Atlanta, nor is the oldest in the group.

6. Neither the painter nor the carpenter is from Dallas.

7. The plumber and the one from Shreveport are into fiction or poetry, in some order.

8. The one from Atlanta is definitely not into drama; and the one from Miami is definitely not into poetry.

ANSWER ON PAGE 122

LOGIC GRID 21

Gallery Theft

Four paintings were stolen from an art gallery a week ago, each one created in a specific style—impressionist, cubist, surrealist, and minimalist—and finished in a specific year in the 1950s—1954, 1955, 1957, or 1958 (but not necessarily in the same order). The painters were from four different countries—Italy, Spain, the United States, and Brazil (in some order). Each painting had an identifying mark on the back (to authenticate it in the case of theft)—a cross, a star, a triangle, and a circle.

Can you figure out in which year each type of painting was created, the country of its painter, and its identifying mark, given the following information?

1. The impressionist painting was finished before 1958, but after 1954.

2. The painting finished in 1954 was not the cubist or surrealist one.

3. The 1958 painting did not have either the cross or star symbol.

4. The surrealist painting was not the one finished last.

5. The minimalist painting, which was not painted by someone from Italy, had either the triangle or circle mark behind it.

6. The impressionist and cubist paintings were created by painters in Spain or Brazil, in some order.

7. The American painting bears the triangle symbol and the cubist painting, the circle symbol.

8. The 1955 painting, the painting created by someone in Brazil, and the painting with the cross symbol were actually found on a street corner the day after they were stolen.

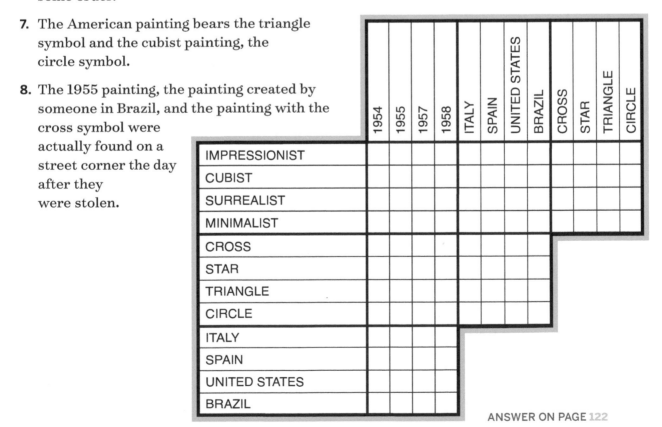

ANSWER ON PAGE 122

LOGIC GRID 22

Doctors

Four doctors, whose names are Tina, Deion, Niesha, and Boris, and whose last names are (in no particular order) Martin, Trainor, Chakra, and Smith, all work in the same medical building. One is a pediatrician, another an oculist, the third an orthopedist, and the fourth an obstetrician (in some order). Each one comes to work in a specific way—walking, bicycle, motorbike, and Vespa (in no particular order).

Can you match the first and last names of each doctor, as well as each one's medical specialty and mode of travel to work, given the following facts?

1. Tina is taller than Dr. Smith but shorter than the oculist, who is not Dr. Martin.

2. Deion is not the tallest, but he is taller than Dr. Chakra.

3. Niesha is also not the tallest.

4. Dr. Trainor is the tallest of the four.

5. Neither Dr. Smith nor Tina nor Deion walk to work.

6. Dr. Martin, the pediatrician, and the obstetrician often meet up on weekends.

7. Tina and the pediatrician come to work either by bicycle or motorbike, in some order.

8. Dr. Smith does not come to work by bicycle.

ANSWER ON PAGE 122

LOGIC GRID 23

Hurricane Names

Several meteorologists got together to come up with names for future hurricanes. They decided on four names from Greek mythology, which they intend to submit to the National Weather Service—Ares, Diana, Artemis, and Hercules. Each name would be assigned to a hurricane in a particular category—Category 1, Category 2, Category 3, and Category 4 (not necessarily in that order). Each name would also be translated into a different language—Spanish, Greek, German, and Italian (again, in no particular order)—and each name would also be assigned a symbol to complete the nomenclature system—a labyrinth design, an Egyptian ankh, a phoenix, and the eye of Horus.

Can you match each hurricane name to its category, the language in which it is to be translated, and the symbol associated with it, given the following information?

1. The name for the Category 4 hurricane is either Hercules or Diana. It was not translated into Greek. Its symbol is not the phoenix.

2. The name for the Category 3 hurricane is not Artemis, and its symbol is not the eye of Horus.

3. The Category 2 hurricane, the hurricane named Hercules, and the hurricane with the ankh symbol were discussed at length.

4. The Category 1 hurricane is not named Artemis or Ares, and it was not translated into Greek.

5. Hercules was not translated into Spanish or Italian. It was not assigned the phoenix or the eye of Horus symbol.

6. The hurricane translated into German was assigned the labyrinth symbol. It was not a Category 4.

7. The hurricane with the ankh symbol was translated into Italian; it was neither a Category 2 nor a Category 4.

	1	2	3	4	SPANISH	GREEK	GERMAN	ITALIAN	LABYRINTH	ANKH	PHOENIX	HORUS
ARES												
DIANA												
ARTEMIS												
HERCULES												
LABYRINTH												
ANKH												
PHOENIX												
HORUS												
SPANISH												
GREEK												
GERMAN												
ITALIAN												

ANSWER ON PAGE 122

LOGIC GRID 24

Flower Lovers

Four longtime friends—Peter, Agatha, Julia, and Sheena—are flower lovers. Each one has been cultivating a certain type of flowering plant for many years—roses, tulips, hortensias, and geraniums (but not necessarily in that order). One friend has been cultivating flowers for 10 years, another for 11, a third for 15, and a fourth for 21 years. Last year, each person gave the flowers as a birthday gift at their birthday—to a brother, a sister, a grandson, and a niece.

Can you figure out what flower each person has been cultivating, for how long, and to whom the flowers were given as a birthday present, based on the following facts?

1. Peter has been cultivating flowers for more than 10 years. He does not have a sister.

2. The one who has been cultivating geraniums for 11 years gave a batch to a niece.

3. The friend who gave flowers to a grandson has been cultivating them for 21 years.

4. The friend who gave flowers to a sister has been cultivating them for less than 21 but more than 10 years.

5. Agatha has also been cultivating flowers more than 10 but less than 21 years.

6. Julia does not have a brother, and she does not cultivate roses.

7. Neither Peter nor Agatha cultivates roses or tulips.

8. The sister of one of the friends has never received roses.

9. Peter cultivates geraniums.

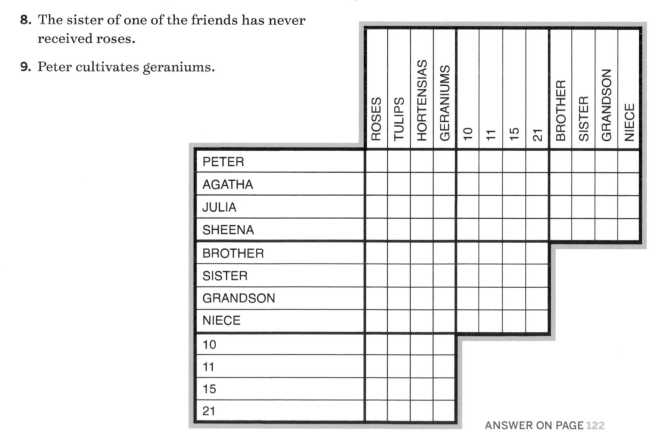

MASYU

TRY THIS!

Make a list of the 10 things that you find hardest to do, like drawing, writing, reading, and so on. Tackle one per week, even if the results are not perfect. Doing so can help break down the barriers to whole-brain functioning.

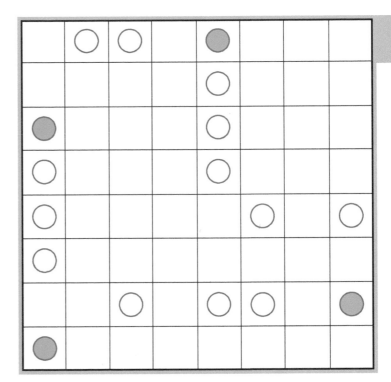

07

ANSWER ON PAGE 122

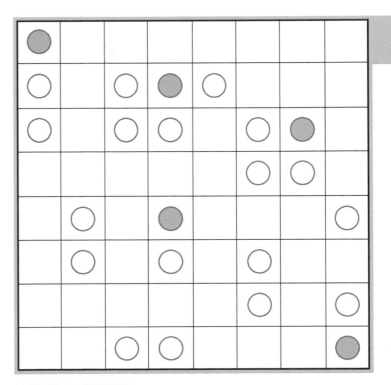

08

ANSWER ON PAGE 123

MASYU

ANSWER ON PAGE 123

TRIVIA CHALLENGE

How many stars and stripes does the American flag have? What do they represent?

ANSWER ON PAGE 123

THE ULTIMATE **BRAIN HEALTH LOGIC PUZZLE BOOK** FOR ADULTS

TRY THIS!

Read a book on logic after solving the puzzles in this book. You will find that what logicians talk about is what you have been doing concretely with puzzle solving.

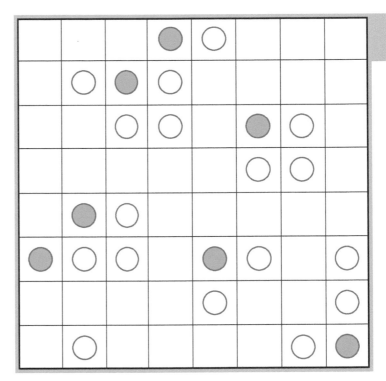

ANSWER ON PAGE 123

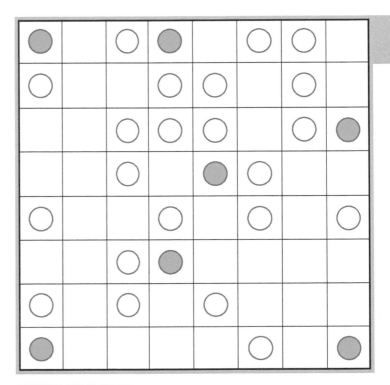

ANSWER ON PAGE 123

NONOGRAM

Grinning Robotic Face

	0	3	9	1 3 2	5 2	5 2	1 3 2	9	3	0
2 2										
8										
2 2 2										
1 2 1										
6										
6										
2 2										
1 1										
6										
4										

ANSWER ON PAGE 123

Apartment Building

	0	9	1 1 1 3	9	2 1 1 1	8	1 1 1 3	9	9	0
2										
8										
1 1 1 2										
8										
1 1 1 2										
8										
1 1 1 2										
8										
3 3										
3 3										

ANSWER ON PAGE 123

Histogram

	0	9	1	4	1	6	1	8	1	3
1										
1 1										
1 1										
1 1 1										
1 1 1										
1 1 1 1										
1 1 1 1 1										
1 1 1 1 1										
9										
0										

ANSWER ON PAGE 123

Iron Formula

	8	1 1	1 1	1	0	7	1 1 1	1 1 1	1 1 1	0
0										
4										
1 4										
1 1										
4 1										
1 4										
1 1										
1 1										
1 4										
0										

ANSWER ON PAGE 123

NONOGRAM

Enclosed Squares

	10	1 1	1 6 1	1 1 1 1	1 1 2 1 1	1 1 2 1 1	1 1 1 1	1 6 1	1 1	10
10										
1 1										
1 6 1										
1 1 1 1										
1 1 2 1 1										
1 1 2 1 1										
1 1 1 1										
1 6 1										
1 1										
10										

ANSWER ON PAGE 124

Camel

	2	5	1	3 1	8	6	5 1	6	2	0
0										
1										
2 3										
2 3										
1 5										
1 6										
8										
1 1										
1 1										
2 2										

ANSWER ON PAGE 124

Umbrella and Raindrops

Column clues: 2 | 2 1 1 | 4 1 | 4 | 10 | 4 1 | 4 3 | 2 1 | 2 1 | 1

Row clues:
- 3
- 5
- 7
- 9
- 1 1 1 1 1
- 1
- 1 1 1
- 1 1 1
- 1 1 1
- 1 3 1

ANSWER ON PAGE 124

Tree

Column clues: 0 | 3 | 4 | 4 1 | 10 | 10 | 4 1 | 4 | 3 | 0

Row clues:
- 2
- 4
- 6
- 8
- 8
- 2 2 2
- 2
- 2
- 2
- 4

ANSWER ON PAGE 124

Denial, Denial

This nonogram puzzle conceals a hidden message. Solve the puzzle first and then you will actually see the secret message appear before your eyes.

	5	1 1 1	0	1	5	1
2 3	T	R	N	K	J	I
1 1	P	X	E	S	Q	T
2 1	M	A	V	A	L	H
1 1	N	X	E	I	M	A
2 1	T	U	R	D	N	T

Hidden Expression: ☐☐☐ ☐☐☐ ☐☐☐☐ ☐☐☐☐

ANSWER ON PAGE 124

CRYPTIC PUZZLE 10

A Body Part

The following sudoku hides an expression. Solve it first and then use the solution to decode the answer. Hint: look for a number-to-letter pattern.

	4	5		3	9	8	7	6
8			7	1	4		3	
	9	3	5			2	1	4
6	5			8	2	3	9	7
9		4	3	5			2	
	3	8	9	7		4		1
3				4	5	7	6	2
4	1		6		7	5	8	
	6			2	3			

Hidden Expression: ☐ ☐ ☐ ☐ ☐ ☐ ☐ ☐

ANSWER ON PAGE 124

CRYPTIC PUZZLE 11

A Favorite Pastime

The following logic grid puzzle conceals a hidden expression. To decode it, you will have to first solve the puzzle and then use the answer to figure out the hidden word.

Four neighbors—Bernice, Letisha, Lola, and Ahmed—often bump into one another. From their conversations, it has become clear that each one has a favorite color—green, maroon, emerald, or aqua, in no particular order—and a favorite number—1, 2, 3, or 4—again, not necessarily in that order.

Can you match each person with their favorite color and number, given the following information?

1. Bernice does not like the number 4, nor the color aqua. Her favorite number is smaller than either Letisha's or Ahmed's favorite number. Letisha and Ahmed also do not like the number 4.

2. The one whose favorite number is 1 loves the color green.

3. Neither Letisha nor Lola loves the number 2. The one who does love this number also loves the color aqua.

4. Letisha lives right next door to the person who loves the color emerald.

5. Letisha does not love the number 4.

	1	2	3	4	GREEN	MAROON	EMERALD	AQUA
BERNICE								
LETISHA								
LOLA								
AHMED								
GREEN								
MAROON								
EMERALD								
AQUA								

Hidden Word: ☐ ☐ ☐ ☐ ☐ ☐ ☐

ANSWER ON PAGE 124

CRYPTIC PUZZLE 12

A Good State of Mind

The hidden word can be decoded only if you solve the calcudoku puzzle first. You will have to figure out the code as well.

P	Y	P	A	H
15x		2	7+	
4		9+	4x	
40x			60x	
		4x		
1-				5

Hidden Word: ☐ ☐ ☐ ☐ ☐

ANSWER ON PAGE 125

CRYPTIC PUZZLE 13

A Math Gem

In this sudoku, rather than a word, there is a hidden sequence that has a specific meaning. To figure out what it is, you will have to solve the puzzle first.

1	8	4		5	6	7		9
		5	2	4	8		3	
		3	9				5	
8	2			3	4	6		7
3	7	6	1				4	
4		9		7	2	3	8	1
		7	8		1	2	6	
6		8	4	2		9		
9	4	2		6	3		1	5

Hidden Sequence: ⬚⬚⬚⬚⬚⬚⬚⬚⬚⬚⬚⬚

ANSWER ON PAGE 125

CRYPTIC PUZZLE 14

Communication Emergency

The following nonogram contains a hidden message, which you can figure out only after solving the puzzle first.

	0	6	3 1	4 1	9	4 1	3 1	6	0
1	C	A	L	L	R	M	E	W	H
3	E	N	Y	S	T	U	O	U	C
5	A	N	V	W	A	L	N	I	T
7	I	I	C	O	L	S	A	R	S
7	V	D	A	N	I	C	H	I	E
1 1 1	R	C	X	X	H	X	X	A	Y
1 1 1	U	R	X	X	L	X	X	U	R
1 1 1	G	C	X	X	I	X	X	A	E
7	N	M	R	C	D	R	P	R	T

Hidden Message: ☐☐☐☐ ☐☐ ☐☐☐☐☐

☐☐☐ ☐☐☐. ☐☐ ☐☐

☐☐☐☐ ☐☐☐☐☐☐

ANSWER ON PAGE 125

CRYPTIC PUZZLE 15

Immigration

By solving the logic grid, you will be able to figure out from which country the great grandparents of the four individuals emigrated, based on a hidden code.

Four individuals—Glenn, Macy, Ulf, and Amin—are the great grandchildren of immigrants, who came to America from the same country. They live in four different cities—Chicago, Buffalo, Miami, and Austin—but not necessarily in that order. Their ages are 21, 22, 23, and 24, again, in no particular order. The years of immigration of their great grandparents to America are: 1946, 1947, 1948, and 1949.

Can you match the individuals with their ages, year of immigration of their great grandparents, and city of residence, given the following facts?

1. Glenn is not the oldest, and he does not live in Buffalo.

2. The oldest lives in Austin. The great grandparents of this individual came to America in 1949.

3. Glenn and the person who lives in Miami are both enrolled in med school.

4. The great grandparents of the individual who lives in Chicago came to America in 1946. That individual is the youngest of the four.

5. Macy does not live in Miami or Buffalo.

6. Ulf also does not live in Buffalo. The 23-year-old does.

7. The great grandparents of the 22-year-old did not immigrate in 1948.

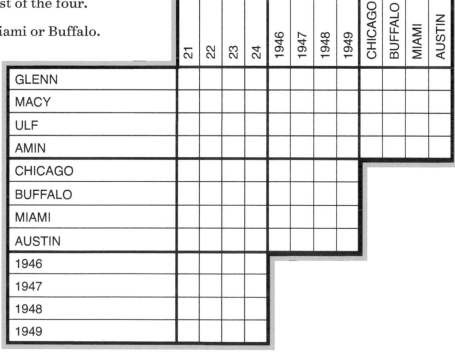

Country of Origin: ☐ ☐ ☐ ☐

ANSWER ON PAGE 125

CRYPTIC PUZZLE 16

Another Puzzle Type

To unravel the hidden word in this masyu, solve the puzzle first, and then try to figure out where the hidden word is.

A	N	O	C	D	E	G
N	T	U	O	T	F	G
R	H	S	D	G	T	U
D	A	R	S	N	C	Y
S	R	T	E	S	R	S
H	G	P	Y	T	A	H
A	G	O	E	S	T	P
Q	R	D	M	T	O	K

Hidden Word: ⬜⬜⬜⬜⬜⬜⬜⬜

ANSWER ON PAGE 125

DIFFICULT PUZZLES

SUDOKU

		3	6			8	1	2
		4	9	5	1	7		
6	1					9	5	4
4	9					6	7	1
7	3			9				
		6	2	1				9
3		8	5	4				7
1				8	2	5	3	
2		5	1		3	4	9	8

ANSWER ON PAGE **126**

DID YOU KNOW?

The frontal lobes of the brain play a key role in many thinking processes. One of these is logic. It's no surprise, therefore, that the kinds of logic puzzles included in this book might help activate those very lobes, which are particularly important for abstract thinking.

8		7		9		3		4
2		9	4		5		1	
	1		7		8		6	2
1	4				9		7	8
3		5		7		2		9
		6	8			5		1
	2		6		7			
6	5	8	9				2	3
9		1	5		3		8	

ANSWER ON PAGE **126**

TRY THIS!

Make a list of the 10 pieces of music that you love and turn it facedown. Leave the list somewhere for a bit. When you come back to it, try to write the list over again on the back side of the paper, comparing it to your original list. This is an effective way to improve memory.

19

		8	7	5	4	1		
			6		2	7		
6		7	3	9		4	8	2
1	2			7	8		9	3
8	9				5	2		7
7		5	2	3	9		1	
			8	4				
		1	5	2			7	4
4		2		1		6		8

ANSWER ON PAGE 126

20

	5		9		1	8		2
8		6	4				9	5
	2	4	8					
4	6				8	2	5	1
1							8	9
	8	9		1	6	3		
2	9			7	4	5	1	3
6		5	1	8		4		
	4		3		5	9		8

ANSWER ON PAGE 126

SUDOKU

21

	7	5		8		1	6	
1		8	5		4	3		9
3	9				7		5	
	6	1		3		5		7
			2		6			1
	3	7		5		2		6
5	8		6		3		2	4
6		2			5	8		3
	1	3	8		2	6	9	

ANSWER ON PAGE **126**

22

7	2	3	1			4	8	5
5	4				8			9
		1	4		7	3	6	
	6	4			3	9	5	
			9	2	4			8
	8	9			5	2	4	7
6	1	5					7	4
4			7	8		5		6
9			5	4		1		

ANSWER ON PAGE **126**

TRIVIA CHALLENGE

How many cities can you name that have canals running through them?

23

7		9		4	2	1	3	6
	6		7	3		4		2
4		3		6		9		8
1	7			9	4		6	3
3		4		1	7			
		6	3		8		1	
5	1			8	3		4	
			4			2		
9			5				8	1

ANSWER ON PAGE **126**

24

7		4		3		2	1	6
	1		2	5	4			
	2					3		4
	6		4	9				1
	4	7			3	9	6	5
3		1		8			7	
1				4	8			
2		9	6		5	1	4	
4	8	5	3	1			9	7

ANSWER ON PAGE **126**

CALCUDOKU

13

Puzzle 13:
3x		1-	6+		6
20x			36x		2÷
	15+		5+		
9+				5	3
		2	90x	5x	
4-		4			

ANSWER ON PAGE 126

TRIVIA CHALLENGE

What type of bird has the largest wingspan of all surviving species?

14

Puzzle 14:
5	12x			72x	3
12+		75x			
			19+	2x	
				5	90x
6x	1	15+			
				2-	

ANSWER ON PAGE 127

15

1	40x	6	48x	2-	
18x					
		1	15x	10+	
21+	5x	2		1	6
		96x	5+		5

ANSWER ON PAGE **127**

16

15x		35x		2-	14+	4
6		3	2			
27+	4x	4	1	15x		6
			60x	17+		
						3
3	14+	7x	6	14x		3-
			8+		1	

ANSWER ON PAGE **127**

CALCUDOKU

112x		36x	4+		30x		
	5			2	24x	7	
3	35x		1			17+	
12x		4					
14+				15x	7	12+	
1	7+		7				
2	210x			4	3x		

ANSWER ON PAGE **127**

10x	7	6+		6	14+		
			7+	4		7	
18x		7		1	40x		
7	30x	7+	1	210x	9+		
			6				
48x		6			7	30x	
	5+		7				

ANSWER ON PAGE **127**

LOGIC GRID 25

The County Fair

Five friends went to the county fair yesterday, which had a mini amusement park. Their names are Lionel, Jorge, Karen, Shandra, and Alex. As it turned out, each one went separately on one ride only—the carousel, the scrambler, the Ferris wheel, the roller coaster, or the rotor (in some order). Each person donned a hat with a specific color—red, brown, yellow, blue, or green. By the way, the friends work at the following places—an office, a factory, a school, a store, and a restaurant.

Can you figure out on which ride each friend went on, what color hat each one wore, and where each one works, based on the following facts?

1. Neither Lionel, the red hat wearer, nor the one who works in an office went on the carousel.

2. Jorge and Karen went on the scrambler and the Ferris wheel, in some order.

3. Shandra did not go on the carousel or roller coaster.

4. The red hat wearer did not go on the scrambler or the Ferris wheel.

5. Karen and the scrambler rider had chocolate ice cream at the fair.

6. The brown hat was not worn by either the roller-coaster rider, the office worker, or the Ferris wheel rider.

7. The brown hat wearer does not work in either a store or restaurant.

8. Alex does not work in a factory.

9. Lionel did not wear either the yellow or the blue hat.

10. The office worker did not wear the blue hat.

11. Neither Lionel nor Karen work in a restaurant.

12. The blue hat wearer does not work in a store.

13. Lionel works in a store.

	CAROUSEL	SCRAMBLER	FERRIS WHEEL	ROLLER COASTER	ROTOR	RED	BROWN	YELLOW	BLUE	GREEN	OFFICE	FACTORY	SCHOOL	STORE	RESTAURANT
LIONEL															
JORGE															
KAREN															
SHANDRA															
ALEX															
OFFICE															
FACTORY															
SCHOOL															
STORE															
RESTAURANT															
RED															
BROWN															
YELLOW															
BLUE															
GREEN															

ANSWER ON PAGE 127

LOGIC GRID 26

Teachers

Jenna, Gill, Harlan, Surina, and Tyrell teach at the same high school. They teach math, history, civics, computer science, and English, in some order. Each one also is involved in running an after-school club—one runs the cooking club, another runs the drama club, a third runs the music club, a fourth the debate club, and a fifth the social justice club. Each teacher graduated from a different East Coast university—Yale, Harvard, Princeton, Columbia, and Rutgers.

   Can you figure out what subject each person taught, what club each one runs, and what university each one graduated from, given the following facts?

1. The Harvard grad does not teach history, but runs either the cooking or social justice club.

2. The Yale grad teaches either English or math, but does not run the debate club or the music club.

3. The Columbia grad, the one who teaches history, and the one who runs the debate club play on the same weekend soccer team.

4. The Princeton grad teaches either civics or computer science. Harlan runs the music club.

5. The Yale grad, the Harvard grad, and the one who teaches math share lunch-hour duties.

6. The Harvard grad, who lives near the computer science teacher, does not teach English.

7. The Rutgers grad does not run the music or cooking club.

8. Neither the history nor English teacher runs the social justice club.

9. Jenna, the Harvard grad, and the one who teaches computer science get to school at about the same time.

10. Jenna also meets up frequently with the teachers who run the music and drama clubs for coffee.

11. Gill did not go to Harvard or Princeton. He has become a close friend of the math teacher.

12. Harlan also did not go to Harvard or Princeton. He has become best friends with Surina, who also did not go to Harvard.

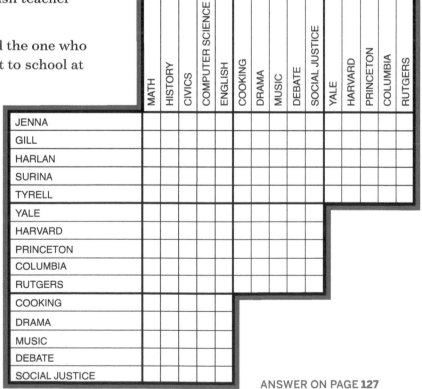

ANSWER ON PAGE 127

LOGIC GRID 27

Math Competition

Students from five countries—Greece, Ethiopia, Egypt, India, and Russia—took the first five prizes in an international math competition in some order. Each country entered the competition on a different day of the week—Monday, Tuesday, Wednesday, Thursday, or Friday (in no specific order). The total amount of time given to finish the test was 7 hours. One country took only 1 hour, another country took 2 hours, a third country took 3 hours, a fourth country took 4 hours, and a fifth country took 5 hours.

Given the following information, can you figure out the prize achieved by each country, on which day each country entered the competition, and how many hours each country took to finish the test?

1. The country placing first did not take the test Monday; nor did the country placing fifth.

2. The countries placing second and third took the test on either Wednesday or Friday (in some order); neither country took 5 hours to complete the test.

3. The country placing first did not take 5 hours to complete the test; the country who took the test on Monday took only 1 hour.

4. The country finishing first did not take the test on Thursday.

5. The second and third place winners took 3 and 4 hours, in some order.

6. The country that took the test on Wednesday and the third place finisher were very happy with the outcome.

7. The country that took the test on Wednesday did not take 4 hours to complete the test.

8. Greece did not finish first or fifth; and it did not enter the competition on Monday or Friday.

9. Ethiopia did not finish third or fourth and it did not take 5 hours to complete the test.

10. Egypt did not finish first or fourth, and did not take 5 hours.

11. India did not enter on Thursday.

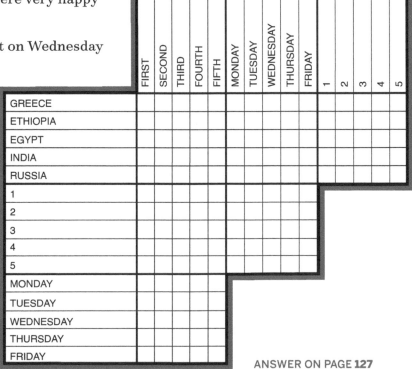

ANSWER ON PAGE 127

LOGIC GRID 28

Forensic Scientists

Five longtime friends are forensic scientists who work for the FBI. Their names are Annie, Bella, Claudia, Darlene, and Eartha. Their last names are Aleman, Barker, Carson, Davies, and Eastman, but not necessarily in that order. Their ages are five years apart—25, 30, 35, 40, 45. Their specific areas of expertise are (in no particular order): fingerprints, DNA, ballistics, bloodstains, and biometrics.

Can you match their first and last names, as well as each person's age and area of expertise, based on the following information?

1. The first letters of the names and last names do not match.

2. Claudia, Ms. Davies, and Ms. Eastman often meet for lunch.

3. Claudia helped Ms. Barker solve a recent case.

4. Bella, Ms. Carson, and Ms. Eastman have solved many cases together.

5. Eartha and Ms. Barker solved a serial killer case together last year.

6. The oldest of the five is either Darlene or Ms. Barker.

7. Annie is younger than Eartha but older than Bella, who is not the youngest.

8. The youngest is a DNA specialist and the oldest the fingerprint specialist.

9. Neither Eartha nor Annie is the ballistics expert.

10. Ms. Barker is not the biometrician.

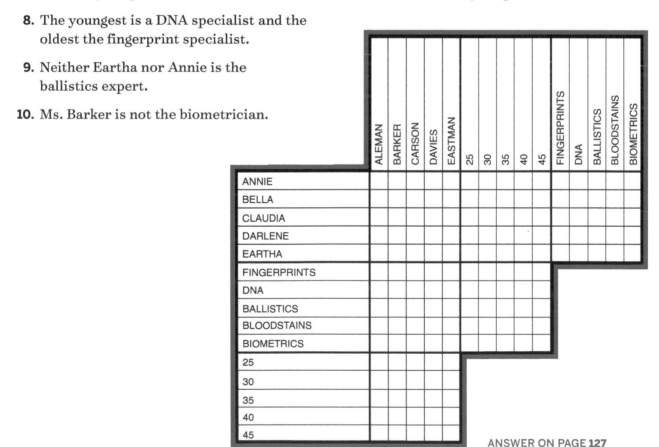

ANSWER ON PAGE 127

LOGIC GRID 29

Recent Graduates

Ronda, Leticia, Gloria, Keisha, and Ada all graduated from the same university. Their majors were, in no particular order, French, architecture, business, economics, and education. While at university, each made a new friend—Emilio, Keshon, Kahlil, Jerry, and Paul (in no particular order). The five students now engage in either running, swimming, fencing, weight lifting, or boxing in no particular order.

Can you match each person with her major, her friend, and the activity she engages in, given the following information?

1. Ronda, the French major, and the architecture major belonged to the same sorority.

2. The economics and education majors did not join any sorority at the university.

3. Leticia, the economics major, and the French major played on the same basketball team.

4. The architecture major never joined any sports team while at university.

5. Ada, Gloria, and the French major graduated summa cum laude.

6. The economics major and Ada were great debaters.

7. Neither the French major nor the architecture major nor the business major keeps fit by swimming.

8. The economics major is into either running or fencing. Gloria is not into fencing.

9. The French and architecture majors are into either boxing or weight lifting in some order.

10. Keisha is not into weight lifting.

11. Neither Keisha nor Ada became friends with Emilio.

12. Gloria and Ronda became friends with Jerry and Paul, in some order.

13. Keshon became friends with the one who is into boxing and Kahlil with the one who is into weight lifting.

14. Paul and the one into running continue to be good friends.

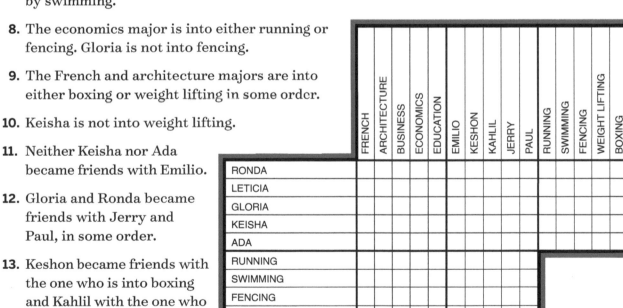

ANSWER ON PAGE **127**

LOGIC GRID 30

Appliance Deals

An appliance store held a one-day sale last week of five items—a refrigerator, a blender, a toaster, a coffee maker, and a dishwasher. Each item had a special tag attached to it to enhance its appeal—Exclusive, Limited, Best, Unique, or Amazing (in no particular order). Each tag was colored in red, purple, orange, yellow, or brown (in some order). Finally, each appliance also came with a special offer—a ticket to a movie, a box of donuts, a dinner-for-two voucher at a local restaurant, a T-shirt, or a baseball glove (again, in no particular order).

Can you match each appliance with its tag, the color of the tag, and the treat it came with, according to the following information?

1. The appliance with the Exclusive tag was not red or brown and did not come with the T-shirt.

2. The appliances with the Limited and Best tags came with the movie ticket and box of donuts, in some order; the tags were colored purple or orange (again, in some order).

3. The appliance with the Unique tag came with either the dinner voucher or the baseball glove; the tag was not colored red or yellow.

4. The appliance with the brown tag did not come with the dinner voucher.

5. The appliance with the purple tag and the appliance with the Best tag were the first two to be sold.

6. The appliance with the orange tag did not come with the movie ticket.

7. The refrigerator did not come with the movie ticket or the donuts, and its tag was not colored brown or red.

8. The blender was not tagged as Best, and it did not come with either the baseball glove or T-shirt.

9. The coffee maker was not tagged as Amazing or with an orange tag.

10. The toaster came with the donuts.

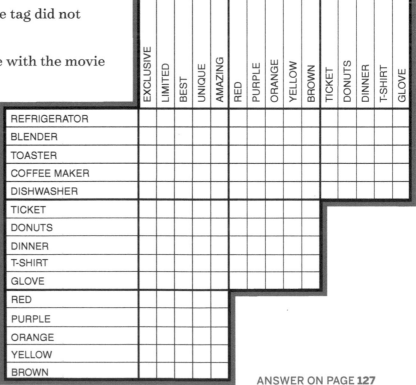

ANSWER ON PAGE **127**

LOGIC GRID 31

Track-and-Field Stars

Five athletes were chosen to represent the United States at an international track-and-field meet last year. Their names were Martha, Nick, Latoya, Kendis, and Juanita. Each person won first prize in either the 100-meter dash, the high jump, the javelin throw, the discus throw, or the weight lifting event (in some order). The athletes came from the following states—Arkansas, Oregon, Wisconsin, Idaho, and Utah (in no particular order). The numbers worn by the athletes on their official jackets were: 4, 5, 7, 15, and 21 (again, in no particular order).

Given the following facts, can you figure out which event each athlete won, what state they came from, and what their number was?

1. The athlete who wore the number 4 did not win the high jump, and did not come from Idaho.

2. The 5 and 7 number wearers won in the javelin and discus throws, but not necessarily in that order.

3. The number 15 wearer won either the weight lifting or 100-meter dash.

4. The number 5 wearer, the number 15 wearer, and the athlete who won the 100-meter dash all stayed in the same complex during the meet.

5. The athlete who won the discus throwing competition and the number 5 wearer came from Arkansas and Oregon, but not necessarily in that order.

6. The winners of the 100-meter dash and the weight lifting competitions came from Idaho and Utah, but not necessarily in that order.

7. The number 7 wearer did not come from Arkansas.

8. Martha did not wear either the number 5 or the number 7, and she did not come from either Idaho or Wisconsin.

9. Latoya did not wear the number 5 or 15, nor did she come from Wisconsin.

10. Neither Kendis nor Nick won the high jump. Kendis is not from Arkansas.

ANSWER ON PAGE 127

LOGIC GRID 32

Lawyers

Five lawyers—Ms. Malik, Mr. Costa, Ms. Arnold, Mr. Long, and Ms. Guilan—are specialists in one of these areas—corporate, criminal, equity, civil, or contract law—in no particular order. The lawyers have been practicing for a different number of years—1, 2, 3, 4, or 5 years. Each lawyer works in a different city—Providence, Memphis, Nashville, Sacramento, or Phoenix.

Can you determine which area each lawyer is practicing in, for how many years, and in what city, given the following facts?

1. The lawyer who has been practicing for 1 year does not work in Providence.

2. The lawyers who have been practicing for 2 and 3 years work in Memphis and Nashville, but not necessarily in that order.

3. The lawyer practicing in Providence is not the one who has been working for 4 years.

4. The lawyer in Phoenix has been practicing for more than 1 year.

5. The lawyer in Sacramento is not the corporate law specialist, nor is the one who has been practicing for 3 years.

6. The Phoenix and Providence lawyers specialize in criminal and equity law, in some order.

7. The lawyer practicing in Nashville is not the civil law or corporate law specialist.

8. The criminal lawyer is not the one who has been working the greatest number of years. The corporate lawyer is not the one who has been working 3 years.

9. Ms. Malik is not the corporate or contract lawyer, nor does she work in Phoenix or Providence.

10. Mr. Costa has not been working for 3 years, and his specialty is neither criminal law nor equity law. He does not work in Sacramento.

11. Ms. Arnold does not practice criminal law and she does not work in Providence.

12. Mr. Long does not practice equity law.

ANSWER ON PAGE **127**

LOGIC GRID 33

Friendly Dinner

Five friends go out together for dinner every Friday night. Their names are Lamar, Don, Mario, Felipe, and Jack. Each person orders the same main dish every time—spaghetti, minestrone, pot roast, dumplings, or vegan skewers (in no particular order). Each one also orders the same type of beverage—wine, beer, juice, a soft drink, or soda water—and the exact same dessert—fruit, cheese, baklava, cheesecake, or banana pudding (all in no particular order).

Can you figure out which dish, beverage, and dessert each friend always has based on the given information?

1. The one who has the spaghetti does not have the wine with it, nor does the friend who has the dumplings.

2. The ones who order minestrone and pot roast have beer and juice with their meal, in some order.

3. The one who orders the dumplings does not have the soft drink with his order.

4. The one who has the soft drink does not have fruit for dessert, nor does the dumplings eater.

5. The ones who have the minestrone and the pot roast have baklava and cheesecake for dessert, in some order.

6. The one who orders spaghetti does not have banana pudding for dessert.

7. The minestrone eater and the one who orders beer live near each other.

8. The one who drinks juice does not have baklava for dessert.

9. Lamar does not have the minestrone or the pot roast, nor does he have the banana pudding or the fruit for dessert.

10. Don does not have beer or soda water with his meal, and he does not have the fruit for dessert.

11. Mario does not have the dumplings or skewers.

12. Felipe does not have the fruit.

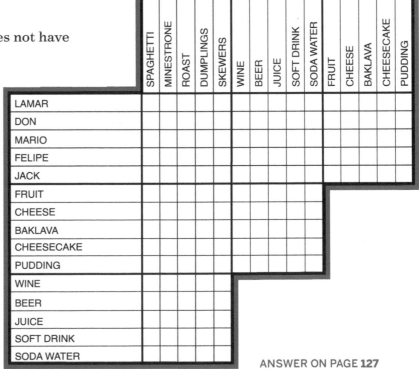

ANSWER ON PAGE **127**

LOGIC GRID 34

All in the Family

The Burton family—mother, father, son, daughter, and live-in grandmother—go by their nicknames, which are, in no particular order: Boo, Roo, Woo, Noo, and Foo. Each one loves a particular type of vegetable—lettuce, cabbage, celery, yams, or beans (in some order). Each one is also a lover of a particular sport—baseball, tennis, curling, golf, or bowling.

Can you match each nickname to kin relation (mother, father, son, daughter, grandmother), type of vegetable loved, and favorite sport, according to the given information?

1. Neither the mother nor the daughter is into curling.

2. The father and son are into baseball and tennis, in some order.

3. The mother is not into golf.

4. The mother, the baseball lover, and the son are early risers.

5. The curling lover does not like lettuce, nor does the son or daughter.

6. The father and son like either cabbage or celery, in some order.

7. The daughter does not like yams, and the tennis player does not like cabbage.

8. Boo, who is not the father or son, does not like yams or beans.

9. Roo, who is not the son or daughter, is not into curling.

10. Woo is not the daughter or grandmother.

11. Noo is not into yams.

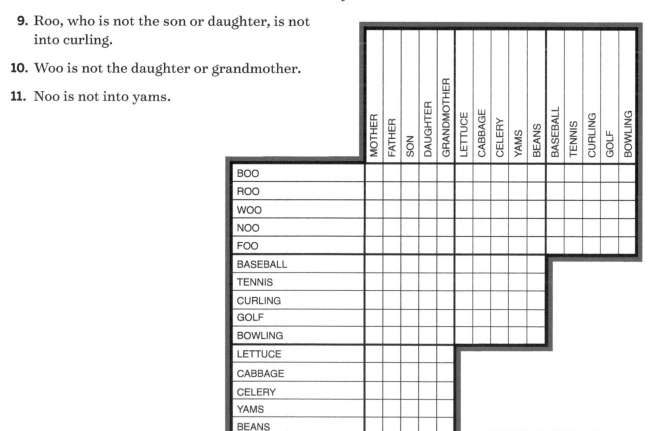

ANSWER ON PAGE 127

LOGIC GRID 35

Dog Lover

Keshawn loves dogs. He has five household dog companions—a golden retriever, a Siberian husky, a bulldog, a French poodle, and a pug. The names he has given to them are, in no particular order, Bella, Lucy, Charlie, Buddy, and Lucky. Each dog sleeps in one specific room of Keshawn's house at night—the pantry, the kitchen, the den, the attic, or Keshawn's bedroom—again, in no particular order. Each dog is taken for a walk at specific times of the evening (after Keshawn gets home from work)—at 6:00, 6:30, 7:00, 7:30, or 8:00.

Can you match each dog companion to its name, sleeping room, and time that it goes on a walk, based on the given information?

1. The retriever is not taken out at 6:00 or 8:00.

2. The dogs taken for a walk at the 6:30 and 7:30 times are the husky and the poodle, but not necessarily in that order.

3. The dog taken out at 8:00 is not the pug.

4. The husky is taken for a walk at a later time than the retriever.

5. The pug does not sleep in the pantry.

6. The retriever and the husky sleep in either the bedroom or the den, in some order.

7. The pug does not sleep in the attic.

8. The dog that goes for a walk at 7:00 sleeps in the den.

9. Bella is not the poodle or the retriever and does not sleep in the bedroom or pantry.

10. Lucy does not sleep in the den or bedroom and she does not go for a walk at 8:00.

11. Charlie is not the husky and does not sleep in the pantry.

12. Buddy is not the bulldog.

13. Bella is taken for a walk at 6:00.

	RETRIEVER	HUSKY	BULLDOG	POODLE	PUG	PANTRY	KITCHEN	DEN	ATTIC	BEDROOM	6:00	6:30	7:00	7:30	8:00
BELLA															
LUCY															
CHARLIE															
BUDDY															
LUCKY															
6:00															
6:30															
7:00															
7:30															
8:00															
PANTRY															
KITCHEN															
DEN															
ATTIC															
BEDROOM															

ANSWER ON PAGE 127

LOGIC GRID 36

Eccentric Hat Collector

Maria loves hats and has a collection of classic hats. Her five favorites, which she displays in her living room prominently, are the fedora, the beret, the boater, the cloche, and the porkpie. She has had each hat for a different number of years—1, 3, 5, 7, and 10 (in no particular order). She has pinned an initial to each hat, each of which has a symbolic meaning for her—the letters A, B, C, D, and E (in some order). She has also wrapped each hat in a colored ribbon—green, violet, indigo, crimson, and yellow.

Can you match each hat with the number of years Maria has owned it, its symbolic letter, and color of ribbon, given the following facts?

1. Maria has not had the green hat for 10 years.

2. The violet and indigo hats have been on display for 3 and 5 years, but not necessarily in that order.

3. She has had the yellow hat for less than 7 years, and the crimson hat for more than 5 years.

4. She really likes the indigo hat, which she has had for less than 5 years.

5. The letter A is not pinned to either the green, indigo, or violet hat; it is pinned, however, to a hat that she has had less than 10 years.

6. She did not pin the letter B to either the violet or the green hat, nor to the hat she has had for 10 years.

7. She has not pinned the D or E to the crimson hat.

8. She has not pinned the D to the green hat.

9. The fedora does not have the letter B or D, and it is not green or crimson.

10. The beret is not violet or green, and it does not bear the letter C.

11. The boater is not green or crimson.

12. Maria had not had the cloche for 10 years.

ANSWER ON PAGE 127

MASYU

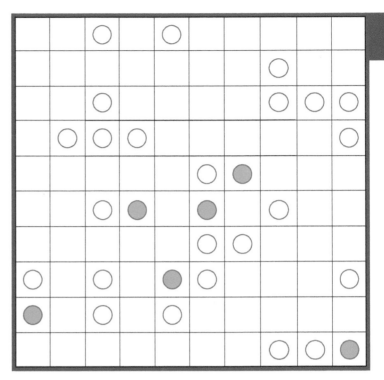

13

ANSWER ON PAGE **127**

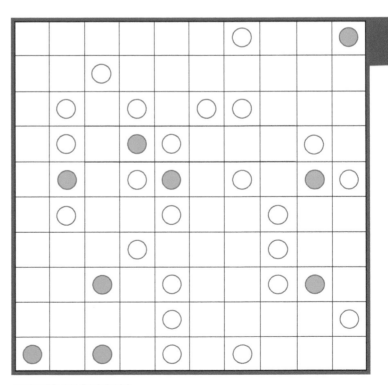

14

ANSWER ON PAGE **128**

MASYU

ANSWER ON PAGE **128**

ANSWER ON PAGE **128**

THE ULTIMATE **BRAIN HEALTH LOGIC PUZZLE BOOK** FOR ADULTS

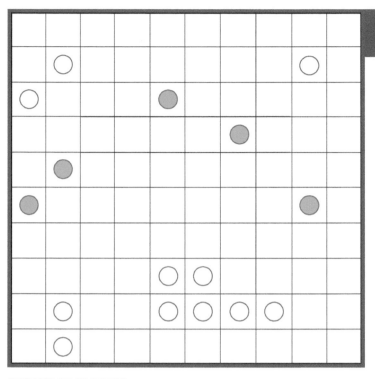

ANSWER ON PAGE **128**

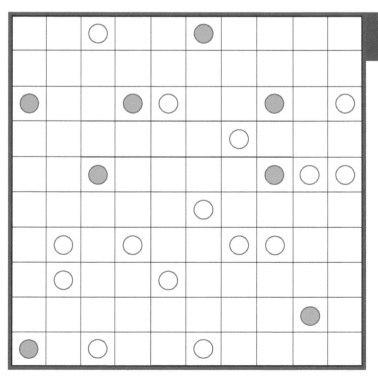

ANSWER ON PAGE **128**

NONOGRAM

Face

	5	2 2	1 1	1 1	1 1 1 1	1 1 2 2 1	1 1 2 2 1	1 2 2 1	1 1 2 2 1	1 1 2 2 1	1 1 1 1	1 1	1 1	2 2	5
5															
2 2															
1 1															
1 3 3 1															
1 1															
1 2 2 1															
1 2 2 1															
1 1 1															
1 1 1															
1 1															
1 7 1															
1 5 1															
1 1															
2 2															
5															

ANSWER ON PAGE **128**

Scary Animal

	0	3	6 1	2 12	5 9	5 5	2 8 1	15	3 9	6	6	6	2 5 1	1 7	13
6															
8															
2 2 2 3															
8 1 1															
6 1															
2 2 1															
9 1															
10 1															
12															
12															
12															
2 8															
2 2 2															
2 2 2															
3 3 3															

ANSWER ON PAGE **128**

THE ULTIMATE **BRAIN HEALTH LOGIC PUZZLE BOOK** FOR ADULTS

House Robot

Column clues: 0, 1, 4/1, 2/2, 3/8, 2/1/8, 2/4/2, 2/4/2, 2/1/8, 3/8, 2/2, 4/1, 1, 0, 0

Row clues:
- 4
- 6
- 1 1
- 1 1
- 1 1
- 2
- 2
- 8
- 10
- 1 2 2 1
- 1 6 1
- 1 6 1
- 2 2
- 3 3
- 5 5

ANSWER ON PAGE **128**

Checkerboard

Column clues: 0, 0, 13, 1 1 1 1 1 1 1 1, 2 1 1 1 1 1 2, 1 1 1 1 1 1 1, 2 1 1 1 1 1 2, 1 1 1 1 1 1 1, 2 1 1 1 1 1 2, 1 1 1 1 1 1 1, 2 1 1 1 1 1 2, 1 1 1 1 1 1 1, 13, 0, 0

Row clues:
- 0
- 11
- 1 1 1 1 1 1
- 2 1 1 1 2
- 1 1 1 1 1 1
- 2 1 1 1 2
- 1 1 1 1 1 1
- 2 1 1 1 2
- 1 1 1 1 1 1
- 2 1 1 1 2
- 1 1 1 1 1 1
- 2 1 1 1 2
- 1 1 1 1 1 1
- 11
- 0

ANSWER ON PAGE **128**

NONOGRAM

House

	1 1	10	3 1	4 2 1	5 2 1	5 1	7 4	7 4	5 1	5 2 1	5 2 1	4 1	3 1	10	1 1
2															
2															
7															
9															
11															
13															
15															
1 1															
1 2 2 1															
1 2 2 1															
1 1															
1 2 1															
1 2 1															
1 2 1															
15															

ANSWER ON PAGE **129**

Repeating Pattern

	2 2	1 1 1 1	1 1 1 1	1 1 1 1	5 5	2	1 1	1 1	5	2 2	1 1 1 1	1 1 1 1	1 1 1 1	5 5
2 2														
1 1 1 1														
1 1 1 1														
1 1 1 1														
5 5														
2														
1 1														
1 1														
1 1														
5														
2 2														
1 1 1 1														
1 1 1 1														
1 1 1 1														
5 5														

ANSWER ON PAGE **129**

Intersecting Figures

ANSWER ON PAGE 129

Puzzle 23

Column clues: 0 | 0 | 9 | 1 1 | 9 1 | 1 1 1 1 | 1 1 1 1 | 1 1 1 1 | 1 1 1 1 | 9 1 1 | 1 1 1 1 1 | 1 1 1 1 1 | 1 1 9 | 1 1 1 1 | 1 9 | 1 1 | 1 1 | 1 1 | 9

Row clues:
- 11
- 1 1
- 11 1
- 1 1 1 1
- 1 1 1 1
- 1 1 1 1
- 1 1 1 1 1 1
- 1 1 1 1 1 1
- 1 1 1 1
- 1 1 1 1
- 1 11
- 1 1
- 1 1
- 11
- 0

Mechanical Dog

ANSWER ON PAGE 129

Puzzle 24

Column clues: 0 | 8 | 14 | 1 2 3 5 | 7 3 | 5 1 3 | 3 3 6 | 13 | 1 10 | 11 | 9 | 10 | 9 | 6 | 6 | 8 | 7 | 7 | 0 | 0

Row clues:
- 1 1
- 1 4 1
- 8
- 9
- 2 2 4 1
- 12 1
- 4 9 1
- 17
- 2 11
- 17
- 17
- 16
- 2 2 2 2
- 2 2 2 2
- 1 1 1 1

CRYPTIC PUZZLE 17

A Get-together

The solution to the following nonogram hides a rebus phrase, that is, a phrase that can be figured out by "reading" the figure in a certain way.

	5	1 1	6	1 5	1	1	6	1 1 6	1 1 2	5
3 3										
1 1										
1 3										
1 1										
1 3										
10										
1 1 1 1										
1 1 1 1										
1 1 1 1										
1 1 1 1										

Rebus Expression: ☐☐☐ ☐☐ ☐☐☐ ☐☐☐☐☐

ANSWER ON PAGE 129

CRYPTIC PUZZLE 18

A Truism

Here is another cryptic based on a rebus code. After solving the masyu puzzle, you will have to figure out the code to come up with the rebus expression.

H	I	S	T	O	R	Y
A	V	R	T	U	O	P
W	V	C	N	P	X	K
E	T	Y	U	R	X	S
M	N	O	X	L	M	N
J	T	R	X	S	U	V
K	L	M	N	O	P	Q
H	I	S	T	O	R	Y

Rebus Expression: ☐ ☐ ☐ ☐ ☐ ☐ ☐

☐ ☐ ☐ ☐ ☐ ☐ ☐ ☐ ☐ ☐ ☐ ☐ ☐

ANSWER ON PAGE 129

CRYPTIC PUZZLE 19

Numbers and Letters Make a Good Pair

First solve the calcudoku puzzle, and then try to refigure out the code that relates the letters on top to the shaded squares. This will give you the hidden rebus expression:

W	H	I	L	E
10x	4x		9+	
		12x	5	
2-	10+			5
			6x	1
3	20x			

Rebus Expression: ▢ ▢ ▢ ▢ ▢ ▢ ▢

▢ ▢ ▢ ▢ ▢

ANSWER ON PAGE 129

CRYPTIC PUZZLE 20

Cards

The shaded cells in the sudoku puzzle hide the rebus answer.

		1	5	6	8	7		4
8	7		4			5	1	6
	4	6	7	1				3
7	1		9	4	5			
4	6		8		1	3	9	7
		8	3	7	6	4	5	1
1	8	7	6		4			5
6		9		5	7	1		
	5	4	1	8	3	6		

Rebus Expression: ☐ ☐ ☐ ☐ ☐ ☐

ANSWER ON PAGE **130**

CRYPTIC PUZZLE 21

Beneath It All

	W	A	T	E	R
N	4x		15x	5	6+
R	10+				
U	5x		32x		3
D		3		2	5x
E	6+		3x		

Rebus Expression: ☐ ☐ ☐ ☐ ☐ ☐ ☐ ☐ ☐ ☐

ANSWER ON PAGE **130**

CRYPTIC PUZZLE 22

See No Evil

Like other cryptic nonograms, the follow-up rebus puzzle can be solved by examining the figures that result from solving the nonogram.

	1 4	0	1 4	0	1 4	0	1 4	0	1 4
1 1 1 1 1									
0									
1 1 1 1 1									
1 1 1 1 1									
1 1 1 1 1									
1 1 1 1 1									
0									

Rebus Expression: ☐ ☐ ☐ ☐

ANSWER ON PAGE 130

CRYPTIC PUZZLE 23

Salutation

This cryptic masyu hides a rebus expression, which you will have to figure out after solving the masyu.

S	R	W	L	K	(G)
F	(O)	U	(B)	N	M
(Y)	R	W	D	A	N
S	A	R	T	R	(O)
A	B	(D)	C	(E)	D
R	T	U	I	O	P

Rebus Expression: ☐ ☐ ☐ ☐ ☐ ☐ ☐

ANSWER ON PAGE 130

CRYPTIC PUZZLE 24

Enjoyment

After solving the following two logic grid puzzles, use the answers to set up a rebus code, relating names and positions in some way. The information to solve each logic grid is given separately, so you will have to solve each one separately before considering the two solutions together to solve the rebus puzzle.

Logic Grid 1

Four friends—Ornella, Orma, Dina, and Ginelle—decided to race one another yesterday. Based on the given information, can you determine in which order they finished?

1. Ornella finished before Dina.

2. Ornella finished after Orma.

3. Ginelle finished ahead of Orma.

	FIRST	SECOND	THIRD	FOURTH
ORNELLA				
ORMA				
DINA				
GINELLE				

Logic Grid 2

Four friends—Elvis, Mack, Tim, and Ivan—also decided to race one another yesterday on another track. Based on the given information, can you determine the order in which each man finished?

1. Elvis finished after Mack.

2. Mack finished after Ivan.

3. Tim finished before Ivan.

	FIRST	SECOND	THIRD	FOURTH
ELVIS				
MACK				
TIM				
IVAN				

Rebus Expression: ☐ ☐ ☐ ☐ ☐ ☐ ☐ ☐

ANSWER ON PAGE 130

ANSWERS

Warm-up

SUDOKU 1

5	3	6	4	9	1	7	2	8
8	4	9	3	2	7	5	6	1
1	2	7	5	8	6	9	3	4
3	8	1	9	6	5	4	7	2
4	9	2	1	7	3	6	8	5
7	6	5	8	4	2	1	9	3
6	7	8	2	5	4	3	1	9
9	1	4	7	3	8	2	5	6
2	5	3	6	1	9	8	4	7

CALCUDOKU 1

5+ 1	4	3 3	16x 2
3 3	6x 1	2	4
2	3	3- 4	1
7+ 4	2	1	3 3

LOGIC GRID 1

Name	Profession	Flavor
Jamila	Lawyer	Vanilla
Rosie	Dentist	Cherry
Gary	Doctor	Pistachio
Desean	Programmer	Chocolate

MASYU 1

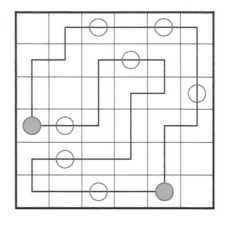

NONOGRAM 1

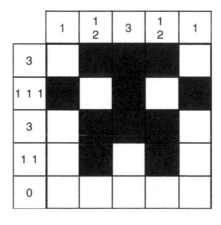

CRYPTIC 1

2	1	4	3	7	8	6	9	5
7	5	3	4	6	9	8	2	1
6	8	9	5	1	2	7	3-M	4
8	3	5	9	2-I	6	1	4	7
1	9	6	7	4	3	5	8	2
4-P	7	2	8	5	1	9	6	3
3	2	1-S	6	8	5-L	4	7	9
9	4	8	1	3	7	2	5	6-E
5	6	7	2	9	4	3	1	8

Code: S = 1, I = 2, M = 3, P = 4,
L = 5, E = 6
Order: 1-2-3-4-5-6
Hidden Word: *simple*

Easy

SUDOKU 2

4	9	7	1	8	3	6	5	2
2	8	1	9	6	5	4	3	7
3	5	6	4	7	2	1	9	8
1	2	9	5	4	7	8	6	3
7	6	5	8	3	9	2	1	4
8	3	4	2	1	6	9	7	5
9	4	3	6	5	8	7	2	1
6	7	8	3	2	1	5	4	9
5	1	2	7	9	4	3	8	6

SUDOKU 3

9	7	8	1	4	5	2	3	6
6	3	2	9	8	7	5	4	1
4	1	5	3	2	6	7	8	9
2	6	7	5	9	8	3	1	4
1	5	4	6	3	2	8	9	7
8	9	3	7	1	4	6	5	2
3	8	9	2	6	1	4	7	5
7	2	1	4	5	3	9	6	8
5	4	6	8	7	9	1	2	3

SUDOKU 4

8	9	3	7	2	4	5	6	1
6	7	1	9	5	8	2	3	4
5	2	4	3	1	6	9	7	8
7	5	6	4	3	1	8	2	9
4	8	9	2	7	5	6	1	3
3	1	2	6	8	9	4	5	7
9	3	5	1	4	2	7	8	6
2	6	7	8	9	3	1	4	5
1	4	8	5	6	7	3	9	2

SUDOKU 5

4	9	5	1	8	6	3	2	7
1	3	7	5	2	9	8	6	4
8	6	2	3	4	7	5	9	1
3	1	8	4	7	2	6	5	9
9	5	6	8	3	1	7	4	2
7	2	4	6	9	5	1	3	8
2	8	3	7	6	4	9	1	5
6	4	1	9	5	8	2	7	3
5	7	9	2	1	3	4	8	6

SUDOKU 6

7	6	4	5	8	2	1	3	9
5	9	3	7	1	6	2	4	8
2	8	1	9	4	3	5	7	6
3	7	6	8	2	9	4	5	1
9	4	5	3	7	1	6	8	2
1	2	8	6	5	4	3	9	7
4	3	2	1	9	7	8	6	5
8	1	9	4	6	5	7	2	3
6	5	7	2	3	8	9	1	4

SUDOKU 7

7	4	2	1	6	9	3	5	8
6	3	9	8	7	5	1	4	2
1	8	5	2	4	3	9	7	6
3	6	1	7	2	8	5	9	4
2	5	4	9	3	6	8	1	7
9	7	8	5	1	4	2	6	3
4	1	3	6	9	2	7	8	5
5	2	7	4	8	1	6	3	9
8	9	6	3	5	7	4	2	1

SUDOKU 8

8	4	2	5	7	9	6	1	3
6	1	5	3	4	8	9	7	2
7	9	3	6	1	2	8	5	4
1	8	6	4	3	7	2	9	5
4	2	7	9	8	5	3	6	1
3	5	9	2	6	1	7	4	8
2	6	1	8	9	4	5	3	7
5	3	4	7	2	6	1	8	9
9	7	8	1	5	3	4	2	6

CALCUDOKU 2

4	1	2	3
3	2	1	4
2	3	4	1
1	4	3	2

CALCUDOKU 3

1	4	2	3
4	3	1	2
2	1	3	4
3	2	4	1

CALCUDOKU 4

4	1	2	3
2	3	4	1
1	2	3	4
3	4	1	2

CALCUDOKU 5

1	2	4	3
4	1	3	2
3	4	2	1
2	3	1	4

CALCUDOKU 6

2	1	4	3
1	2	3	4
4	3	2	1
3	4	1	2

LOGIC GRID 2

Name	Surname	Major
Maria	Wang	History
Shamila	Hoskins	Spanish
Jasmine	Bramish	Physics
Katia	Norabella	Math

LOGIC GRID 3

Name	Age	Shirt Color
Paula	55	Blue
Marco	30	Green
Heather	25	Yellow
Jamil	70	White

LOGIC GRID 4

Item	Price	Bonus
Laptop	$500	Batteries
Mobile device	$705	Ticket
Game	$100	Discount
Watch	$250	Warranty

LOGIC GRID 5

Athlete	Medal	Country
Gymnast	Silver	Greece
Runner	Platinum	Italy
Wrestler	Gold	Zambia
Swimmer	Bronze	Slovakia

LOGIC GRID 6

Coin	Value	Country
Roman	$3 million	France
Greek	$1 million	Belgium
Sumerian	$4 million	Algeria
Chinese	$2 million	Peru

LOGIC GRID 7

Car	Prize	Color
Dodge	Second	Green
Chevrolet	Third	Black
Studebaker	Fourth	Blue
Ford	First	Silver

LOGIC GRID 8

Name	Surname	Specialization
Paula	Sanji	Neurology
Kayla	Gorski	Podiatry
Derek	Garcia	Urology
Leroy	Troy	Cardiology

LOGIC GRID 9

Name	Coffee	Pastry
Nakia	Americano	Danish
Darlene	Mocha	Éclair
Kamira	Macchiato	Croissant
Shauna	Espresso	Strudel

LOGIC GRID 10

Name	Emblem	Racket
Tamika	Bear	Power
Brenda	Lion	Tweener
Juri	Tiger	Control
Nimish	Deer	Modern

Pairs: Tamika-Brenda, Juri-Nimish

LOGIC GRID 11

Name	Placement	Coach
Austin	First	Blaise
Chicago	Third	Jake
Tulsa	Fourth	Kristina
Reno	Second	Maria

LOGIC GRID 12

Name	Animal	Music
Gurdeep	Cat	Rock
Lana	Turtle	Jazz
Keshawn	Gerbil	Classical
Pina	Dog	Rap

MASYU 2

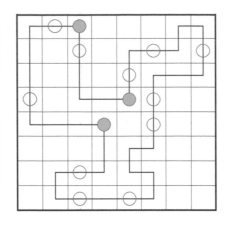

MASYU 3

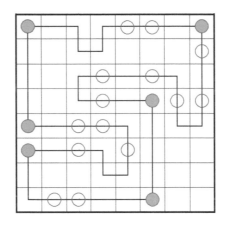

MASYU 4

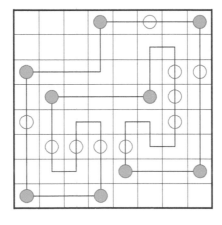

MASYU 5

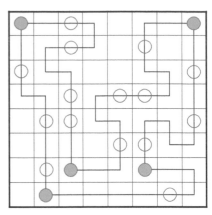

MASYU 6

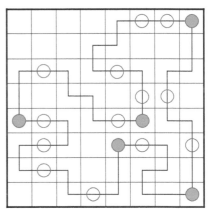

NONOGRAM 2

NONOGRAM 3

NONOGRAM 4

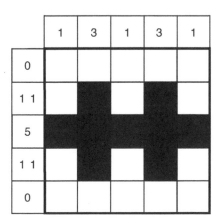

NONOGRAM 5

NONOGRAM 6

NONOGRAM 7

NONOGRAM 8

CRYPTIC 2

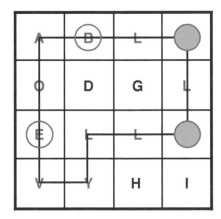

Code: Each letter on the side of the puzzle corresponds to the first number in the row. So, the letter in the first row is E and the number in the first cell of that row is 4. So, E is the fourth letter in the hidden word.
E = 4, M = 3, G = 1, A = 2
Order: 1-2-3-4 = G-A-M-E
Hidden Word: *game*

CRYPTIC 3

The nine letters that the lines cross are (starting at the top and going around the grid): L-B-A-O-E-V-Y-L-L-L. Rearranging these produces the hidden word.
Hidden Word: *volleyball*

CRYPTIC 4

Name	Order
Artemis	Second
Ahmed	Fourth
Keisha	First
Reina	Third
Ella	Sixth
Troy	Fifth

Code: The order of each person, when laid out, is, from first to last in the line: Keisha, Artemis, Reina, Ahmed, Troy, Ella. Take the first letter of each name in this order to spell the required word: KARATE.
Hidden Word: *karate*

CRYPTIC 5

The nonogram figure is the salutation "hi." The figure blocks out irrelevant letters, leaving those that make up the hidden word. The top two letters in the second column are "B-E"; the two letters below them are "G-I"; and in the fourth column, the letters are "N-N-I-N-G." Stringing these together, we get the hidden word.
Hidden Word: *beginning*

CRYPTIC 6

Code: Each letter on top corresponds to the first number in the cell below it: U = 3, E = 4, L = 2, B = 1; in order: 1-2-3-4 = B-L-U-E. Each letter on the side corresponds to the shaded number in the row: N = 4, O = 2, M = 1, O = 3; in order: 1-2-3-4 = M-O-O-N.
Hidden expression: *blue moon*

CRYPTIC 7

The squares not used in the solution, reading from top to bottom, left to right, spell the hidden word.
Hidden Word: *caterpillar*

CRYPTIC 8

Name	Job	Age
Becky	Painter	23
Angela	Artist	24
Lina	Researcher	25
Letisha	Karate instructor	26

Take the ages in ascending order of the four people: Becky-23, Angela-24, Lina-25, Letisha-26. From this order, take the first letters of the names to spell BALL. Now put the jobs in order of the ages of each person: Painter-23, Artist-24, Researcher-25, Karate instructor-26. From this order, take the first letters of the names to spell PARK. Put the two together to get the hidden word.
Hidden Word: *ballpark*

Medium

SUDOKU 9

5	3	2	4	8	6	1	7	9
7	6	9	1	2	3	5	8	4
4	8	1	5	7	9	3	6	2
9	4	3	7	6	2	8	1	5
8	1	7	9	4	5	2	3	6
6	2	5	3	1	8	9	4	7
2	5	4	8	3	7	6	9	1
3	7	6	2	9	1	4	5	8
1	9	8	6	5	4	7	2	3

SUDOKU 12

6	5	3	8	7	2	1	9	4
9	1	8	6	4	3	7	2	5
4	7	2	5	9	1	3	6	8
5	3	7	2	8	6	4	1	9
1	9	6	7	3	4	5	8	2
8	2	4	1	5	9	6	7	3
7	6	9	4	2	5	8	3	1
2	8	5	3	1	7	9	4	6
3	4	1	9	6	8	2	5	7

SUDOKU 15

2	6	8	5	7	1	9	3	4
5	3	7	4	9	8	2	1	6
9	4	1	2	6	3	8	5	7
7	9	2	3	5	6	4	8	1
4	8	3	1	2	7	5	6	9
1	5	6	9	8	4	3	7	2
3	2	9	7	1	5	6	4	8
8	7	4	6	3	2	1	9	5
6	1	5	8	4	9	7	2	3

SUDOKU 10

4	7	8	1	6	5	3	9	2
1	5	9	3	8	2	7	6	4
2	3	6	9	4	7	8	5	1
7	4	5	2	1	6	9	8	3
8	1	3	5	9	4	6	2	7
9	6	2	8	7	3	1	4	5
6	8	7	4	5	1	2	3	9
3	9	4	7	2	8	5	1	6
5	2	1	6	3	9	4	7	8

SUDOKU 13

1	8	3	4	9	7	5	6	2
6	5	4	3	2	1	8	7	9
7	2	9	5	6	8	4	1	3
8	4	2	1	5	9	7	3	6
5	6	1	7	4	3	9	2	8
3	9	7	6	8	2	1	5	4
9	3	5	2	7	4	6	8	1
2	7	8	9	1	6	3	4	5
4	1	6	8	3	5	2	9	7

SUDOKU 16

1	7	2	6	8	9	3	5	4
6	4	5	7	2	3	1	8	9
8	9	3	1	5	4	7	6	2
5	2	1	3	7	6	4	9	8
9	3	7	8	4	2	6	1	5
4	6	8	9	1	5	2	3	7
7	1	6	2	9	8	5	4	3
3	8	4	5	6	7	9	2	1
2	5	9	4	3	1	8	7	6

SUDOKU 11

7	5	9	4	6	3	1	8	2
4	6	3	2	8	1	9	7	5
1	2	8	7	5	9	6	3	4
8	9	6	5	4	2	3	1	7
5	1	4	6	3	7	2	9	8
3	7	2	9	1	8	5	4	6
6	8	1	3	7	5	4	2	9
2	3	5	8	9	4	7	6	1
9	4	7	1	2	6	8	5	3

SUDOKU 14

4	1	6	2	5	9	3	8	7
7	3	9	4	8	1	2	6	5
8	2	5	7	3	6	9	1	4
3	5	8	6	2	4	7	9	1
2	7	1	8	9	5	6	4	3
6	9	4	3	1	7	8	5	2
5	8	3	1	6	2	4	7	9
1	6	7	9	4	3	5	2	8
9	4	2	5	7	8	1	3	6

CALCUDOKU 7

9+ 4	5	7+ 2	3 3	6+ 1
48x 3	2	1	4	5
2	4	200x 5	4+ 1	3
3x 1	3	4	5	2
5 5	1	1- 3	2	4 4

CALCUDOKU 8

5 (15+)	**4** (4)	**1** (6x)	**2**	**3**
3	**5**	**2**	**4** (4)	**1** (15x)
2 (2)	**1** (6x)	**4** (4)	**3**	**5**
1 (12x)	**2**	**3**	**5** (5)	**4** (12+)
4	**3**	**5**	**1**	**2**

CALCUDOKU 9

3 (18x)	**1**	**2**	**4** (7+)	**5** (5)
5 (5)	**4** (60x)	**3**	**2**	**1**
4 (11+)	**3**	**1**	**5**	**2** (6x)
2	**5**	**4** (4)	**1**	**3**
1 (1)	**2** (7+)	**5**	**3** (12x)	**4**

CALCUDOKU 10

1 (7+)	**4** (14+)	**2**	**3** (3)	**5** (20x)
2	**3**	**5**	**1** (1)	**4**
4	**2** (8x)	**3** (3)	**5** (8+)	**1**
5 (2-)	**1**	**4**	**2**	**3** (5+)
3	**5** (5)	**1** (4x)	**4**	**2**

CALCUDOKU 11

2 (16x)	**5** (20x)	**1**	**4**	**3** (9+)
4	**2**	**5** (2-)	**3**	**1**
3 (15x)	**1** (8+)	**4** (4)	**2** (4x)	**5**
5	**4**	**3**	**1**	**2**
1	**3** (3)	**2** (40x)	**5**	**4**

CALCUDOKU 12

5 (12+)	**3** (12x)	**4**	**2** (30x)	**1** (1)
4	**1**	**2** (2)	**5**	**3**
1	**2**	**3** (8+)	**4**	**5** (12+)
2 (6x)	**5** (100x)	**1**	**3** (3)	**4**
3	**4**	**5**	**1**	**2**

LOGIC GRID 13

Name	Surname	Film Genre	Sport
Helena	Darah	Thriller	Tennis
Francine	Soto	Horror	Hockey
Quisha	Moore	Comedy	Golf
Kana	Lee	Spy	Swimming

LOGIC GRID 14

Surname	Field	Hobby	Order
Adebe	Physics	Painting	Fourth
Gemelli	Chemistry	Chess	Third
Kang	Medicine	Gardening	First
Aetos	Biology	Checkers	Second

LOGIC GRID 15

Name	Color	Instrument	Treat
Patricia	Silver	Guitar	Peanuts
Fiona	Blue	Violin	Tarts
Frank	Red	Piano	Chips
Rashon	Gold	Cello	Candy

LOGIC GRID 16

Sport	Year	Coach	Name
Baseball	Sophomore	Lopez	Rockets
Football	Freshman	Chu	Stars
Soccer	Junior	Williams	Jets
Basketball	Senior	Arnand	Suns

LOGIC GRID 17

Name	Art	Language	Dance
Bertha	Music	French	Swing
Shuping	Painting	Greek	Samba
Jamara	Ceramics	Russian	Tango
Ines	Sculpture	German	Waltz

LOGIC GRID 18

Name	Game	Tell	Item
Katia	Spoons	Wiggle	Bracelet
Sarah	Poker	Glance	Ring
Jovan	Blackjack	Touch	Scarf
Sam	Rummy	Scratch	Hat

LOGIC GRID 19

Name	Place	Culture	Season
Doreen	Australia	Cuisine	Summer
Anita	Europe	Art	Winter
Kayla	Asia	Fashion	Spring
Justin	Africa	Music	Fall

LOGIC GRID 20

Name	Trade	City	Literature
Harriet	Painter	Atlanta	Biography
Bill	Plumber	Miami	Fiction
Jason	Electrician	Dallas	Drama
Medina	Carpenter	Shreveport	Poetry

LOGIC GRID 21

Style	Year	Country	Mark
Impressionist	1955	Spain	Star
Cubist	1958	Brazil	Circle
Surrealist	1957	Italy	Cross
Minimalist	1954	United States	Triangle

LOGIC GRID 22

Name	Surname	Specialty	Travel
Tina	Chakra	Obstetrician	Bicycle
Deion	Martin	Orthopedist	Vespa
Niesha	Smith	Pediatrician	Motorbike
Boris	Trainor	Oculist	Walking

LOGIC GRID 23

Name	Category	Language	Symbol
Ares	3	Italian	Ankh
Diana	4	Spanish	Horus
Artemis	2	Greek	Phoenix
Hercules	1	German	Labyrinth

LOGIC GRID 24

Name	Flower	Years	Receiver
Peter	Geraniums	11	Niece
Agatha	Hortensias	15	Sister
Julia	Tulips	21	Grandson
Sheena	Roses	10	Brother

MASYU 7

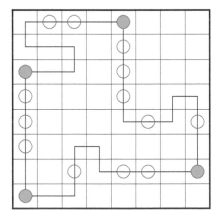

MASYU 8

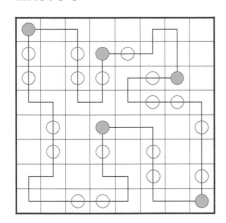

MASYU 11

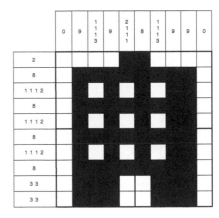

NONOGRAM 10

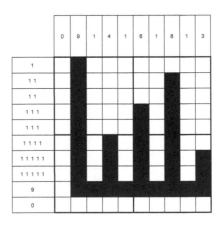

MASYU 9

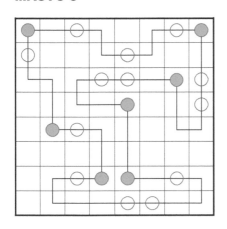

MASYU 12

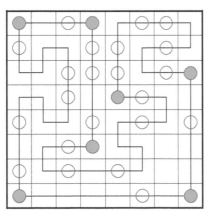

NONOGRAM 11

MASYU 10

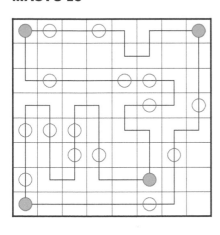

NONOGRAM 9

NONOGRAM 12

NONOGRAM 13

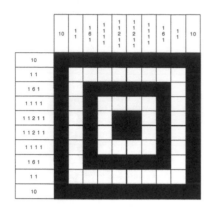

NONOGRAM 14

NONOGRAM 15

NONOGRAM 16

CRYPTIC 9

The nonogram figure spells "ET" (in black). The figure blocks out the letters in the cells it covers. Of the remaining cells, there are two cells marked X. These are discarded from the solution. That leaves three columns of readable letters, top down: N-E-V-E-R; S-A-I-D; T-H-A-T. Together they give the hidden expression.
Hidden Expression: *Never said that*

CRYPTIC 10

Code: The numbers correspond to the alphabet characters in order: 1 = A, 2 = B, 3 = C, 4 = D, 5 = E, 6 = F, 7 = G, 8 = H, and 9 = I. So, the highlighted numbers from the top, left to right, to the bottom, 1-2-9-7-8-5-1-4, stand for the following letters: A-B-I-G-H-E-A-D. These constitute the hidden expression.
Hidden Expression: *A big head*

CRYPTIC 11

Name	Color	Number
Bernice	Green	1
Letisha	Maroon	3
Lola	Emerald	4
Ahmed	Aqua	2

The favorite numbers in order, with their respective believers, are:
1 = Bernice, 2 = Ahmed, 3 = Letisha, 4 = Lola. Taking the first letters of the names in this order gives a part of the solution: BALL. Now, putting the favorite colors in order, we get: 1 = Green, 2 = Aqua, 3 = Maroon, 4 = Emerald. Taking the first letters of the colors in this order gives the second part of the solution: GAME.
Hidden Word: *ballgame*

CRYPTIC 12

	P	Y	P	A	H
	15x 1	5	2 2	7+ 3	4
	4 4	3	9+ 5	4x 2	1
	40x 5	1	3	60x 4	2
	2	4	4x 1	5	3
	1- 3	2	4	1	5 5

Code: Each letter on top corresponds to the number in the shaded cell. So the letter in the first column corresponds to the number in the shaded cell, which is 3. Thus, that letter is the third letter in the hidden word. Reasoning in this way, we get: P = 3, Y = 5, P = 4, A = 2, H = 1.
Rearranging the letters in numerical order: 1-2-3-4-5 = H-A-P-P-Y
Hidden Word: *happy*

CRYPTIC 13

1	8	4	3	5	6	7	2	9
7	9	5	2	4	8	1	3	6
2	6	3	9	1	7	4	5	8
8	2	1	5	3	4	6	9	7
3	7	6	1	8	9	5	4	2
4	5	9	6	7	2	3	8	1
5	3	7	8	9	1	2	6	4
6	1	8	4	2	5	9	7	3
9	4	2	7	6	3	8	1	5

The shaded numbers from top to bottom, left to right, form a sequence: 314159265358, which constitutes the first digits of the number pi (π) when a decimal point is added. That is the answer.
Hidden Sequence: Pi (π) = 3.14159265358 . . .

CRYPTIC 14

	0	6	3 1	4 1	9	4 1	3 1	6	0
1	C	A	L	L		M	E	W	H
3	E	N	Y				O	U	C
5	A	N						I	T
7	I								S
7	V								E
1 1 1	R		X	X		X	X		Y
1 1 1	U		X	X		X	X		R
1 1 1	G		X	X		X	X		E
7	N								T

Code: The solution to the nonogram produces the figure of the façade of a house with a chimney on top and two windows. As in other cryptic nonograms, the letters not covered by the figure are the letters in the message, but the squares with Xs do not fit in. The letters are, reading from left to right, down a row at a time:
C-A-L-L-M-E-W-H-E-N-Y-O-U-C-A-N-I-T-I-S-V-E-R-Y-U-R-G-E-N-T.
Arranging them into words produces the hidden message.
Hidden Message: *Call me when you can. It is very urgent.*

CRYPTIC 15

Name	City	Age	Year
Glenn	Chicago	21	1946
Macy	Austin	24	1949
Ulf	Miami	22	1947
Amin	Buffalo	23	1948

The code involves setting up the immigration order: 1946-Glenn, 1947-Ulf, 1948-Amin, 1949-Macy. The first letters provide the name of the country of immigration of the great grandparents.
Country of origin: *Guam*

CRYPTIC 16

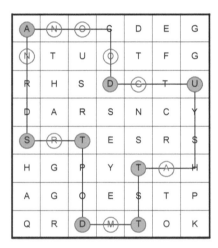

The letters of the hidden word are those in the white circle cells, from left to right, top-to-bottom: N-O-N-O-G-R-A-M.
Hidden Word: *nonogram* ("another puzzle type," of course)

Difficult

SUDOKU 17

9	5	3	6	7	4	8	1	2
8	2	4	9	5	1	7	6	3
6	1	7	3	2	8	9	5	4
4	9	2	8	3	5	6	7	1
7	3	1	4	9	6	2	8	5
5	8	6	2	1	7	3	4	9
3	6	8	5	4	9	1	2	7
1	4	9	7	8	2	5	3	6
2	7	5	1	6	3	4	9	8

SUDOKU 20

3	5	7	9	6	1	8	4	2
8	1	6	4	3	2	7	9	5
9	2	4	8	5	7	1	3	6
4	6	3	7	9	8	2	5	1
1	7	2	5	4	3	6	8	9
5	8	9	2	1	6	3	7	4
2	9	8	6	7	4	5	1	3
6	3	5	1	8	9	4	2	7
7	4	1	3	2	5	9	6	8

SUDOKU 23

7	5	9	8	4	2	1	3	6
8	6	1	7	3	9	4	5	2
4	2	3	1	6	5	9	7	8
1	7	5	2	9	4	8	6	3
3	8	4	6	1	7	5	2	9
2	9	6	3	5	8	7	1	4
5	1	2	9	8	3	6	4	7
6	3	8	4	7	1	2	9	5
9	4	7	5	2	6	3	8	1

SUDOKU 18

8	6	7	2	9	1	3	5	4
2	3	9	4	6	5	8	1	7
5	1	4	7	3	8	9	6	2
1	4	2	3	5	9	6	7	8
3	8	5	1	7	6	2	4	9
7	9	6	8	4	2	5	3	1
4	2	3	6	8	7	1	9	5
6	5	8	9	1	4	7	2	3
9	7	1	5	2	3	4	8	6

SUDOKU 21

4	7	5	3	8	9	1	6	2
1	2	8	5	6	4	3	7	9
3	9	6	1	2	7	4	5	8
2	6	1	9	3	8	5	4	7
8	5	4	2	7	6	9	3	1
9	3	7	4	5	1	2	8	6
5	8	9	6	1	3	7	2	4
6	4	2	7	9	5	8	1	3
7	1	3	8	4	2	6	9	5

SUDOKU 24

7	5	4	8	3	9	2	1	6
6	1	3	2	5	4	7	8	9
9	2	8	7	6	1	3	5	4
5	6	2	4	9	7	8	3	1
8	4	7	1	2	3	9	6	5
3	9	1	5	8	6	4	7	2
1	7	6	9	4	8	5	2	3
2	3	9	6	7	5	1	4	8
4	8	5	3	1	2	6	9	7

SUDOKU 19

2	3	8	7	5	4	1	6	9
9	1	4	6	8	2	7	3	5
6	5	7	3	9	1	4	8	2
1	2	6	4	7	8	5	9	3
8	9	3	1	6	5	2	4	7
7	4	5	2	3	9	8	1	6
5	6	9	8	4	7	3	2	1
3	8	1	5	2	6	9	7	4
4	7	2	9	1	3	6	5	8

SUDOKU 22

7	2	3	1	6	9	4	8	5
5	4	6	2	3	8	7	1	9
8	9	1	4	5	7	3	6	2
2	6	4	8	7	3	9	5	1
1	5	7	9	2	4	6	3	8
3	8	9	6	1	5	2	4	7
6	1	5	3	9	2	8	7	4
4	3	2	7	8	1	5	9	6
9	7	8	5	4	6	1	2	3

CALCUDOKU 13

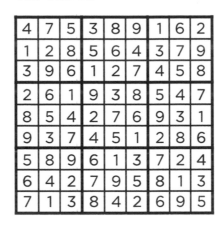

3x 1	3	1- 5	6+ 2	4	6 6
20x 5	1	36x 6	3	2	2+ 4
4	15+ 5	3	5+ 1	6	2
9+ 2	6	1	4	5 5	3 3
3	4	2 2	90x 6	5x 1	5
4- 6	2	4 4	5	3	1

CALCUDOKU 14

5	6	1	2	4	3
4	2	5	1	3	6
6	5	3	4	2	1
3	4	2	6	5	1
2	1	4	3	6	5
1	3	6	5	2	4

CALCUDOKU 15

1	2	6	4	5	3
3	4	5	6	2	1
2	3	1	5	6	4
4	5	2	3	1	6
6	1	4	2	3	5
5	6	3	1	4	2

CALCUDOKU 16

1	3	5	7	2	6	4
6	5	3	2	4	7	1
7	2	4	1	5	3	6
5	1	2	3	6	4	7
2	7	6	4	1	5	3
3	4	1	6	7	2	5
4	6	7	5	3	1	2

CALCUDOKU 17

7	4	2	3	1	6	5
4	5	3	6	2	1	7
3	7	5	1	6	4	2
6	2	1	4	7	5	3
5	1	6	2	3	7	4
1	3	4	7	5	2	6
2	6	7	5	4	3	1

CALCUDOKU 18

1	7	4	2	6	3	5
2	5	1	3	4	6	7
6	3	7	4	1	5	2
7	6	5	1	3	2	4
5	1	2	6	7	4	3
3	4	6	5	2	7	1
4	2	3	7	5	1	6

LOGIC GRID 25

Name	Ride	Color	Work
Lionel	Roller coaster	Green	Store
Jorge	Scrambler	Yellow	Office
Karen	Ferris wheel	Blue	Factory
Shandra	Rotor	Red	Restaurant
Alex	Carousel	Brown	School

LOGIC GRID 26

Name	Subject	Club	University
Jenna	English	Cooking	Yale
Gill	History	Drama	Rutgers
Harlan	Math	Music	Columbia
Surina	Comp sci	Debate	Princeton
Tyrell	Civics	Social justice	Harvard

LOGIC GRID 27

Country	Placement	Day	Hours
Greece	Second	Wednesday	3
Ethiopia	First	Tuesday	2
Egypt	Third	Friday	4
India	Fourth	Monday	1
Russia	Fifth	Thursday	5

LOGIC GRID 28

Name	Surname	Years	Specialty
Annie	Barker	35	Bloodstains
Bella	Davies	30	Ballistics
Claudia	Aleman	25	DNA
Darlene	Eastman	45	Fingerprints
Eartha	Carson	40	Biometrics

LOGIC GRID 29

Name	Major	Friend	Activity
Ronda	Business	Jerry	Fencing
Leticia	Education	Emilio	Swimming
Gloria	Economics	Paul	Running
Keisha	French	Keshon	Boxing
Ada	Architecture	Kahlil	Weight lifting

LOGIC GRID 30

Appliance	Tag	Color	Treat
Refrigerator	Exclusive	Yellow	Dinner
Blender	Limited	Purple	Ticket
Toaster	Best	Orange	Donuts
Coffee maker	Unique	Brown	Glove
Dishwasher	Amazing	Red	T-shirt

LOGIC GRID 31

Athlete	Event	State	Number
Martha	Dash	Utah	4
Nick	Javelin	Arkansas	5
Latoya	Discus	Oregon	7
Kendis	Weight	Idaho	15
Juanita	High jump	Wisconsin	21

LOGIC GRID 32

Lawyer	Specialization	Years	City
Malik	Civil	1	Sacramento
Costa	Corporate	2	Memphis
Arnold	Contract	3	Nashville
Long	Criminal	4	Phoenix
Guilan	Equity	5	Providence

LOGIC GRID 33

Name	Dish	Beverage	Dessert
Lamar	Spaghetti	Soft drink	Cheese
Don	Minestrone	Juice	Cheesecake
Mario	Pot roast	Beer	Baklava
Felipe	Dumplings	Soda water	Pudding
Jack	Skewers	Wine	Fruit

LOGIC GRID 34

Nickname	Relation	Vegetable	Game
Boo	Mother	Lettuce	Bowling
Roo	Father	Cabbage	Baseball
Woo	Son	Celery	Tennis
Noo	Daughter	Beans	Golf
Foo	Grandmother	Yams	Curling

LOGIC GRID 35

Name	Breed	Room	Walk Time
Bella	Pug	Kitchen	6:00
Lucy	Poodle	Attic	6:30
Charlie	Retriever	Den	7:00
Buddy	Husky	Bedroom	7:30
Lucky	Bulldog	Pantry	8:00

LOGIC GRID 36

Hat	Years	Letter	Ribbon
Fedora	1	A	Yellow
Beret	3	B	Indigo
Boater	5	D	Violet
Cloche	7	E	Green
Porkpie	10	C	Crimson

MASYU 13

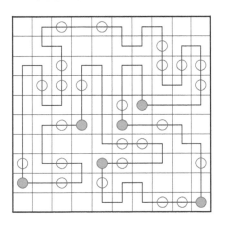

MASYU 14

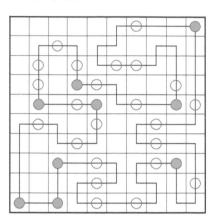

MASYU 17

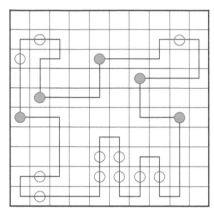

NONOGRAM 18

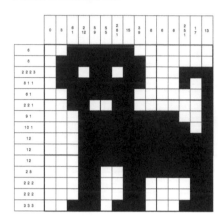

MASYU 15

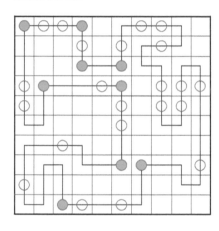

MASYU 18

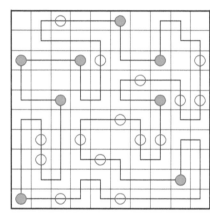

NONOGRAM 19

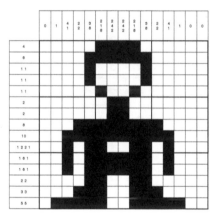

MASYU 16

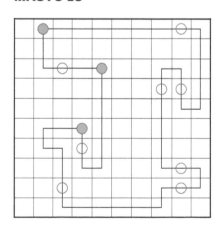

NONOGRAM 17

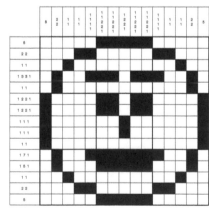

NONOGRAM 20

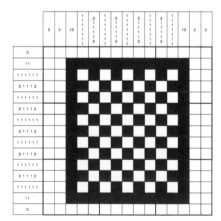

NONOGRAM 21

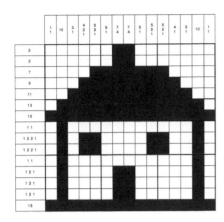

NONOGRAM 22

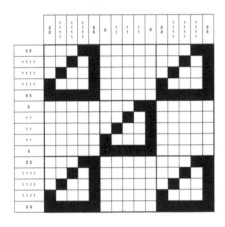

NONOGRAM 23

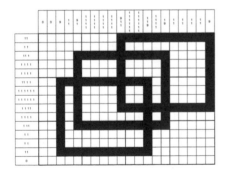

NONOGRAM 24

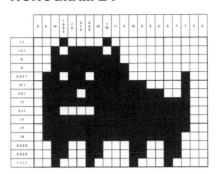

CRYPTIC 17

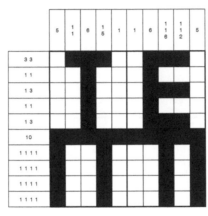

The nonogram figure can be read as TE on a table. With a little adjustment the answer is: *tea on the table*.

CRYPTIC 18

H	I	S	T	O	R	Y
A	V	R	T	U	O	P
W	(V)	C	(N)	P	X	K
(E)	T	Y	U	R	X	S
M	N	O	X	L	M	(N)
J	T	(R)	X	S	(U)	V
K	L	M	N	O	P	Q
H	I	S	T	O	R	Y

Code: The letters not on the circuit, when read from left to right, in the top and bottom row, produce the word "History" twice: History-History. Eliminating the four *X*'s we get the rebus expression.
Rebus Expression: *History repeats itself*

CRYPTIC 19

W · H · I · L · E

10x 5	4x 1	4	9+ 2	3
1	2	12x 3	5 5	4
2- 2	10+ 3	1	4	5 5
4	5	2	6x 3	1 1
3 3	20x 4	5	1	2

Code: The number "1" is shaded in each column. By inserting the 1s into the letters on top, we get: WH11111ILE or W11111HILE, etc. This can be read as "ones in a while" or, with an adjustment, "once in a while," which is the rebus expression.
Rebus Expression: *once in a while*

CRYPTIC 20

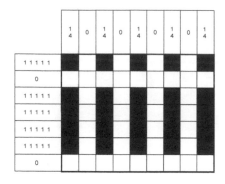

The shaded numbers are all 2s; in cards they are called deuces. Since the clue in the title is "Cards," the rebus answer is deuces.
Rebus Expression: *deuces*

CRYPTIC 21

W A T E R

N	4x 4	1	15x 3	5 5	6+ 2
R	10+ 3	2	5	1	4
U	5x 1	5	32x 2	4	3 3
D	5	3 3	4	2 2	5x 1
E	6+ 2	4	3x 1	3	5

Each shaded cell tells us the position of the letter on the side in the hidden word: N = 2, R = 5, U = 1, D = 3, E = 4. In order: 1-2-3-4-5: U-N-D-E-R. Since this word is UNDER the top word, which is WATER, we get the rebus phrase.
Rebus Expression: *under water*

CRYPTIC 22

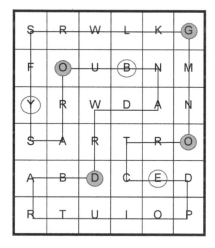

The black figures that result from solving the nonogram are: "i i i i i," which can be read as "i's" = EYES. That is the rebus expression.
Rebus Expression: *eyes*

CRYPTIC 23

In this masyu, the letters that are found in the cells with dark circles are: G-O-O-D. The letters that are found in the cells with white circles are: B-Y-E. Together they produce the rebus expression.
Rebus Expression: *goodbye*

CRYPTIC 24

Female	Position
Ornella	Third
Orma	Second
Dina	Fourth
Ginelle	First

Male	Position
Elvis	Fourth
Mack	Third
Tim	First
Ivan	Second

From the order in which each female finished, and taking the initial letter of the names, we get the word GOOD:
First = Ginelle, Second = Orma, Third = Ornella, Fourth = Dina
= G-O-O-D
From the order in which each male finished, and taking the initial letter of the names, we get the word TIME:
First = Tim, Second = Ivan, Third = Mack, Fourth = Elvis = T-I-M-E
Together they produce the rebus expression.
Rebus Expression: *good time*

Trivia

Page 13: China, India, United States
Page 15: femur (thighbone)
Page 32: Asia
Page 37: kidneys
Page 38: neutron, electrons, protons
Page 47: red
Page 51: about 3 pounds
Page 66: 50 stars (current 50 states) and 13 stripes (original 13 colonies)
Page 85: Venice, Amsterdam, Hamburg, Amiens, Bruges, Tigre, Alappuzha, Birmingham, Suzhou, Gold Coast, Fort Lauderdale
Page 86: the wandering albatross

ACKNOWLEDGMENTS

First and foremost, I wish to thank my editor at Callisto, Annie Choi, for all her help, advice, and excellent suggestions. I must also thank my wonderful wife, Lucia, for putting up with me during the writing of this book. Any infelicities that it may contain are my sole responsibility.

ABOUT THE AUTHOR

 **Marcel Danesi** is professor emeritus of anthropology at the University of Toronto and a co-director of the Cognitive Science Network at the Fields Institute for Research in Mathematical Sciences. He has published extensively on puzzles, both academically and practically. He writes a blog about puzzles for *Psychology Today*.

CPSIA information can be obtained
at www.ICGtesting.com
Printed in the USA
JSHW021216210522
26037JS00001B/2